Preface

The **Trust for the Study of Adolescence (TSA)**, is an independent research organisation and registered charity based in Brighton. It was founded in 1989 to help improve the lives of young people and families. Its work is derived from the belief that there is a lack of knowledge and understanding about adolescence and young adulthood. The Trust is trying to close this gap through: research; training for professionals and parents; projects that develop professional practice; publications for parents, professionals and young people; and influencing policy-makers, service providers and public opinion.

Currently TSA's main areas of work are communication, emotional well-being, health, parenting and family life, social action and youth justice. In addition to research, TSA has an active conference and training programme, and a thriving publications department.

Dr. John Coleman, OBE, Director of TSA, has been the author of all the previous editions of this publication. He was the Editor of the Journal of Adolescence from 1984-2000, and has published many books on this topic, including the widely known textbook "The Nature of Adolescence" (3rd Edn. Routledge, 1999). In the past two years he has written "Sex and Your Teenager" (Wiley, 2002), and is the joint author with Debi Roker of "Supporting Parents of Teenagers" (Jessica Kingsley, 2001). He acts as an advisor to a number of government agencies, and is a member of the Independent Advisory Group for the Teenage Pregnancy Unit. In 2000 he received an award from the British Psychological Society for his Distinguished Contribution to Professional Psychology.

Jane Schofield is currently PA to the Director and acted as researcher for the 2001 edition of Key Data on Adolescence. She previously worked for 10 years as a teacher both in the UK and abroad. She has a long-standing interest in child development and youth issues and believes that having up-to-date and comprehensive information about this age group is essential for policy-makers and other professionals.

1003807096

Key Data on
Adolescence

By John Coleman and Jane Schofield

2003

 Trust for the

 Study of

 Adolescence

Published by the Trust for the Study of Adolescence – TSA

© The Trust for the Study of Adolescence Ltd 2003

TSA Publishing Ltd.

23 New Road, Brighton, BN1 1WZ

Tel: +44 (0)1273 693311

Fax: +44 (0)1273 679907

Email: info@tsa.uk.com

Website: www.tsa.uk.com

British Library Cataloguing-in-Publication Data.
A catalogue record for this book is available from the British Library.

ISBN 1 871504 48 1

Design: Helen Beauvais
Printed by: Creative Media Colour Ltd. Tel: 01273 421966

Contents

Chapter 4: Sexual Health

Sexual Health

Chapter 5: Mental Health

Mental Health

Chapter 6: Crime

Crime

Introduction

Introduction to the 4th Edition of Key Data on Adolescence

It is now six years since the first edition of this text was published by TSA. When the idea was first developed, we saw this book as a resource for students, journalists, researchers, policy-makers and others looking for answers to important questions about the lives of young people in Britain today. Looking back over the last six years, it seems a reasonable conclusion to draw that our initial aim has been met. The succeeding editions of this text have been purchased by a wide variety of professional groups interested in adolescence, and the book has come to be seen as a reliable and up-to-date source of information on young people. However it is of interest to note that much has changed since the first edition of **Key Data on Adolescence** appeared. For one thing other authors and organizations have produced not dissimilar publications, such as **Social Focus on Young People** produced by the Stationery Office in 2000, and **The Well-being of Children in the UK** by Jonathan Bradshaw, published by Save the Children and the University of York in 2002. Furthermore there is much greater interest in adolescence among policy-makers and politicians today than was the case in 1997. Since the Labour Government came to power in May of that year a wide range of new initiatives and policy directives have come into force, encouraging a more sustained focus on the lives of young people. Many of these are mentioned in this 4th Edition of **Key Data on Adolescence.**

Alongside these developments we must place the fact that both the social circumstances and the behaviour of young people have changed over the course of this six year span since 1997. As we note in this edition of our book, there are striking alterations in some indices of risk behaviour, such as alcohol consumption and rates of sexually transmitted infections. Information on mental health also gives cause for considerable anxiety, especially in relation to increases in suicide rates for young men in some parts of the UK. On the other hand conception rates among young women may be starting to decrease, and there are some other "good news" stories, such as the improvements in A level performance, the increased recall of health education information, and the fact that British pupils score higher on educational attainment tests than their counterparts in other European countries.

There is a continuing need for this publication, and we hope it will take its place in research centres, in offices and on library shelves as a regular digest of reliable information charting the changing circumstances of young people's lives in Britain today. In selecting information to include in this publication we are governed, broadly speaking, by three questions. First, have there been changes over time in respect of a particular variable? Is alcohol consumption, or smoking, going up or down? Has the number of young people in the labour force continued to decline? Second, are there individual differences in respect of a particular behaviour or achievement? Do girls perform better than boys in examinations at all levels? Are members of one ethnic group more likely to attend university than members of other ethnic groups? Third, are there regional or national differences in behaviours? Does Scotland have higher suicide rates than other parts of the UK? Do young people in Britain smoke more than young people in other European countries?

We hope that this fourth edition proves as useful as previous editions to all our readers.

We would like to conclude this Introduction by acknowledging the help and assistance of all our colleagues at TSA, in particular those in the research team who have provided us with invaluable leads to new information, those in the training and development team, who remind us of the value of the publication for practitioners, and those in publications, who work so hard to sell this book. We thank them all.

John Coleman
Jane Schofield

Chapter 1

Population, Families and Households

1.1 Population in the UK, 2001

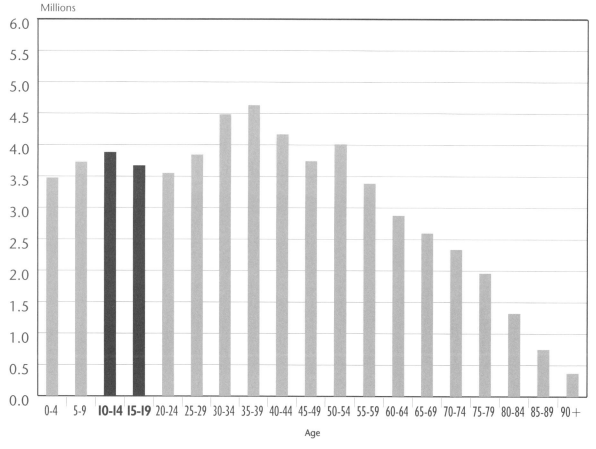

Millions

SOURCE: Office for National Statistics, General Register Office for Scotland, Northern Ireland Statistics and Research Agency.

Population

In any consideration of young people in society we have to keep in mind the population figures. As can be seen in **Chart 1.1** there are approximately 7.5 million teenagers currently living in the United Kingdom. Of these nearly 3.9 million are between the ages of 10 and 14, whilst there are 3.6 million between the ages of 15 and 19. Children under 10 number approximately 7.2 million, so there are slightly more adolescents than children in the population at present. It should be noted that there has been a gradual increase in the number of teenagers over the last decade, together with a corresponding decrease in the number of children. For example in 1995 there were 7.6 million children, but only 7.0 million teenagers in the United Kingdom, a somewhat different picture to the one we see today. The increase in the number of adolescents clearly has important implications for policy, as well as for the provision of those public services, such as education, which are directed towards this age group.

If comparisons are made with older age bands it can be seen that the numbers are significantly higher in the age range 30 to 39, where there are a total of 9.1 million persons. It should also be noted that children and teenagers make up a quarter of the total population of the United Kingdom, roughly similar to other European countries. However, in countries in the developing world the child and adolescent population is more likely to be a half of the total, or even more in some parts of Africa and South America.

1.2 Population by gender and age in the UK, 1901-2000

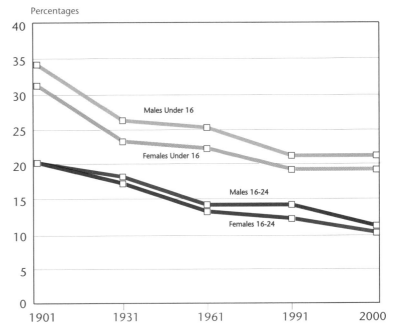

SOURCE: Social Trends 32: 2002 edition. Office for National Statistics.

1.3 Population by ethnic group, 2000-01

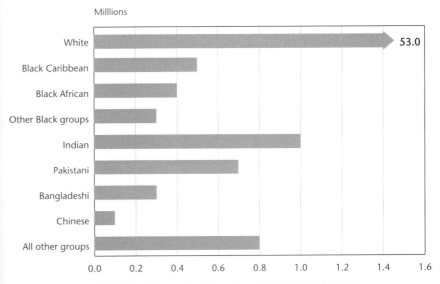

SOURCE: Social Trends 32: 2002 edition. Office for National Statistics.

1.4 Population by age and ethnic group, 2000-01

Percentages

	Under 16	16-34	35-64	65 & over	All ages (=100%) (Millions)
Ethnic Minority groups					
Black	34	30	31	5	1.3
Indian	23	31	38	7	1.0
Pakistani/Bangladeshi	37	36	23	4	0.9
Other groups	30	34	33	3	0.8
White	20	25	39	16	53.0

SOURCE: Social Trends 32: 2002 edition. Office for National Statistics.

As far as historical change is concerned, it can be seen from **Chart 1.2** that the proportion of under-24 year-olds has fallen sharply during the century. The most marked fall has been in the proportion of the population under 16, which for males has fallen from 34% to 21%, while the proportion for females has fallen from 31% to 19%. By contrast the proportion of the population over 75 has risen among males from 1% to 5%, and among females from 2% to 9%. Again these demographic trends have major implications for public policy, and as the demand for services for the over-75s grows, so it becomes more difficult to find resources to meet the needs of those at the other end of the age spectrum.

Turning to race and ethnicity, we can see from **Chart 1.3** that ethnic minority groups accounted for approximately 4 million out of a total population of 57.1 million in 2001. In proportional terms this means that 7% of the population comes from an ethnic minority background. If these figures are analysed more closely, however, it can be seen that there are important differences between ethnic groups. As is apparent from data in **Chart 1.4** there are wide variations in the age distribution of different populations. This is most marked in the Pakistani/Bangladeshi population, where 37% of the population is under 16, as compared with 20% in the white community. Such figures have considerable significance for education and family life. It should be noted that this trend continues with the 16-34 age band, but gradually evens out among older groups. In the oldest group, however, the distribution is reversed, with the white community having a significantly higher proportion of its population over 65. 16% of white people are over 65, in contrast to between 3% and 7% of the ethnic minority population.

Families and Households

During the last thirty years a number of trends in relation to families and households have become apparent in most Western countries. These trends include a decrease in the stability of marriage, and an increase in partnerships and parenthood outside marriage. These trends, as might be expected, have had profound effects on children and young people. The change in family composition between 1971 and 2000 is shown clearly in **Chart 1.5**. Here it can be seen that the number of families with dependent children headed by a lone parent has increased from 8% of all families in 1971 to 26% of all families in 2000. This reflects a major social change, and one that has implications not only for childcare and the welfare state, but also for the very nature of parenthood. Haskey (2002) reports that 2.9 million children were living in families headed by a lone parent in Britain in 2000, and that in that year this figure represented 23% of all dependent children in the country.

Turning now to divorce, it is striking that, while the number of lone parent families has been increasing, the rates of divorce have remained relatively stable since 1985. As can be seen in **Chart 1.6**

1.5 Proportion of families with dependent children headed by a lone parent in Britain, 1971-2000

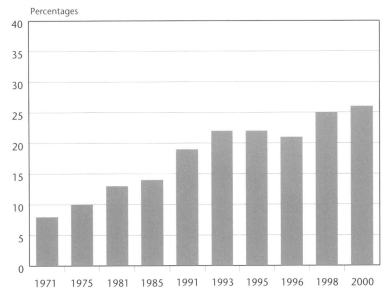

SOURCE: General Household Survey, Living in Britain 2000. Office for National Statistics.

1.6 Rates of divorce per thousand married population in England and Wales, 1985-2000

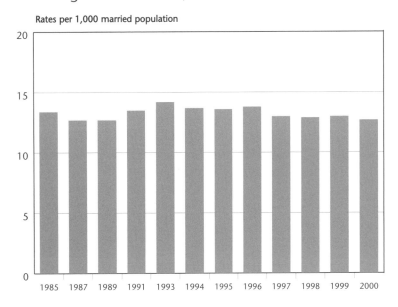

SOURCE: Marriage, divorce and adoption statistics - Series FM2 no 28. Office for National Statistics.

1.7 Families with dependent children headed by lone parents, by circumstance, 1971-2001

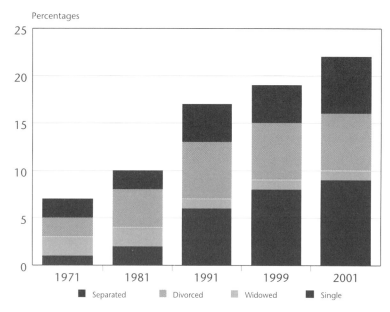

SOURCE: Social Trends No 32: 2002 edition. Office for National Statistics.

1.8 Gross weekly income by family type in Britain, 2000

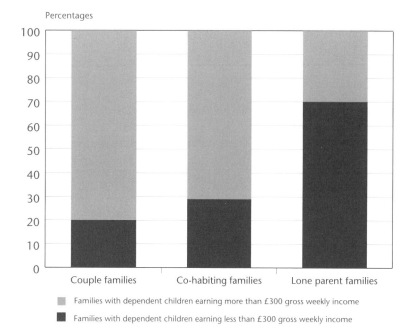

SOURCE: General Household Survey, Living in Britain 2000. Office for National Statistics.

rates of divorce have fluctuated somewhat, but have stayed between 12.7 and 14 per thousand. The increase in lone parent families is explained if we take into account that not all such families originate as a result of divorce. Figures in **Chart 1.7** illustrate this fact. Here it can be seen that single and separated groups have increased markedly since the 1980s.

The present Labour Government has made much of its commitment to cut child poverty, and there is no doubt that this needs to be a key feature in any programme which seeks to improve the quality of life for families in this country. A dramatic illustration of the link between poverty and family type may be found if average household incomes are compared. In **Chart 1.8** we have drawn a distinction between families with weekly incomes over and under £300. As can be seen couple families are nearly three times more likely to have weekly incomes over £300 than are lone parent families. The scale of the problem is further illustrated in **Chart 1.9**, showing the number of children in the UK living in families where neither parent is in work. The numbers of such families have been falling over the last decade, but there were still approximately 2 million children living in workless families in 2002.

Another very important social change that has been occurring since the beginning of the 1980s is the increase in the number of children being born outside marriage. Commentators differ on the specific reasons for this, and it is not clear exactly what reflection this has on present attitudes to marriage.

Undoubtedly many children born outside marriage will be born to parents living in stable partnerships, which may in time turn into marriages. The high numbers of children born outside marriage may not necessarily indicate that marriage is out of fashion. Rather many couples may now wait before getting married, and then find that becoming a parent is the spur that makes them feel that they are ready to marry. Figures in **Chart 1.10** illustrate the growing number of children who are born outside marriage.

Another reflection of the altering nature of the family is the variety of family types in which children now grow up. As a result of the changes we have been discussing, more and more children are likely to spend some time living with a step parent. Actual figures are hard to obtain, but the latest data we have identified are those which appeared in "Social focus on families" (1999). These data are illustrated in **Chart 1.11**, and show that approximately 7.3% of all families with dependent children were step families. This represented somewhere in the region of one million children, and there may be a further one million children and young people who experience part-time step family arrangements.

1.9 Children in workless households in the UK, 1992-2002

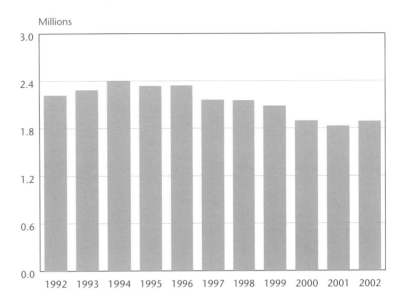

SOURCE: Labour Force Survey, Spring Quarter, ONS 2002.

1.10 Births outside marriage, England and Wales, 1971-2001

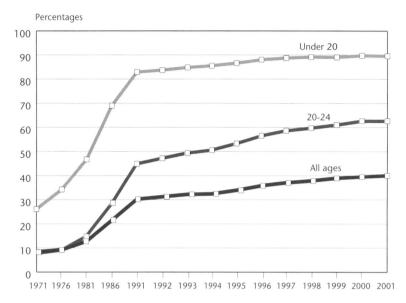

Percentages

SOURCE: Population Trends 108, Summer 2002. Office for National Statistics.

The last question to be considered in this section is that of leaving home. There is general agreement that young people are staying at home longer than was the case in previous generations, for reasons that we will consider in Chapter 2 when we look at the changing nature of the labour market, and the lengthening of the period of further and higher education. Figures provided in Social Trends 30 (2000) indicating the number of young adults remaining in the family home allowed a comparison between the years 1977/78 and 1998/99. These are illustrated in **Chart 1.12**, and demonstrate a trend to staying at home longer, most markedly in young women aged 20-24, and in men aged 25-29.

Comparisons of numbers staying in the family home across various European countries have become available since the 2001 edition of "Key data on adolescence". A study by Maria Iacovou (2002) shows that rates in Britain, although high, are not nearly as high as in southern European countries such as Italy, Spain, and Portugal. To take one example, while 65% of young men in Britain aged 20-24 are still living in the family home, in Spain this figure is 94%. Some of these comparisons are illustrated in **Charts 1.13** and **1.14**. Similar cross-European comparisons may also be found in Iacovou and Berthoud (2001).

1.11 Stepfamilies and families with dependent children, 1991-1993

	Percentages
Married couple stepfamilies	
Stepfather/natural mother	4.3
Stepmother/natural father	0.5
Stepfather/stepmother	0.2
All married couple stepfamilies	5.0
Cohabiting couple stepfamilies	
Stepfather/natural mother	2.0
Stepmother/natural father	0.2
Stepfather/stepmother	0.1
All cohabiting couple stepfamilies	2.3
Lone parent families	20.9
Couple families with natural children only	71.8
All families with dependent children	100

SOURCE: Social Focus on Families. Office for National Statistics.
© Crown Copyright.1999.

1.12 Those living in the parental home in England, by age and gender, 1977/8 and 1998/9

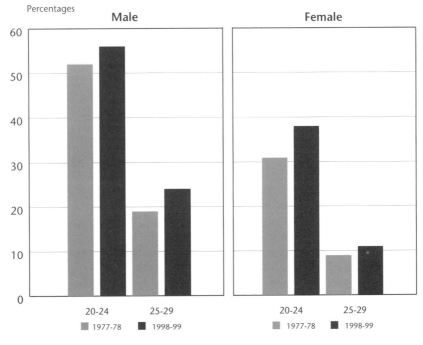

SOURCE: Social Trends, 30.   Office for National Statistics.

1.13 Percentage of young women living at home in different European countries, 1996

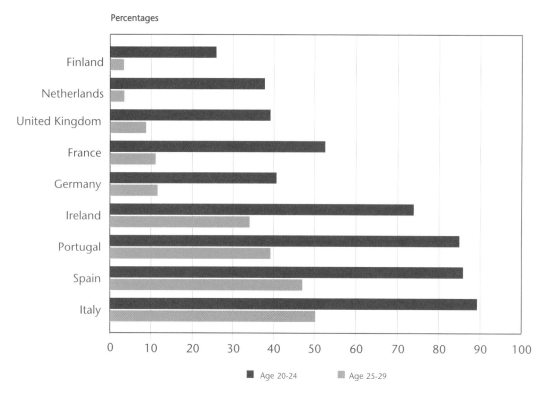

SOURCE: Iacovou (2002).

1.14 Percentage of young men living at home in different European countries, 1996

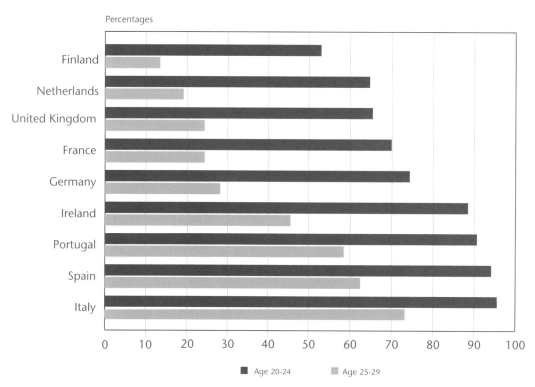

SOURCE: Iacovou (2002).

Children and young people in care/looked after

Although the numbers may be relatively small, children and young people looked after by local authorities are a significant minority, perhaps most importantly because of their vulnerability. Because of this they have rightly received special attention in the last few years. In terms of the statistics, figures are based on a snapshot over a census week, and we will return to the interpretation of these data below. Although there was a steady reduction among the looked after population during the mid-1990s, this trend has now been reversed, as can be seen in **Chart 1.15**. From 60,000 in 1991 the number went down to 49,000 in 1994, but has now risen again to nearly 59,000. We can also look at these trends by considering rates per 10,000. These show a similar picture, in that rates were 55 per 10,000 in 1991, went down to 45 per 10,000 in 1994, and have increased again to 52 per 10,000 in 2001. As Berridge (2002) and Bradshaw (2002) have pointed out, the interpretation of these figures is complex. Various factors are at work here, and a snapshot figure may not fully reflect the whole picture. Factors that need to be considered are the number looked after over a year, which is going down; and the average length of stay in local authority care, which is going up. It seems probable that it is this last factor which is leading to an increase in both the rates and actual numbers of looked after children and young people.

1.15 Children in care/looked after in England, 1991-2001

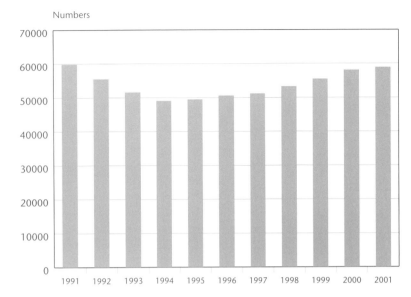

SOURCE: A/F 01/12: Children looked after by local authorities, year ending 31 March 2001. Department of Health.

1.16 Children in care/looked after in England, by gender, 1991-2001

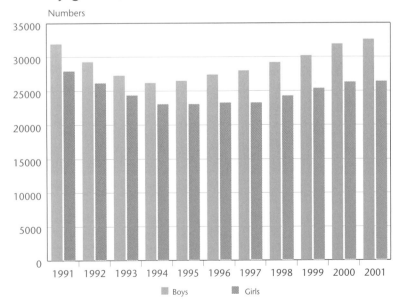

SOURCE: A/F 01/12: Children looked after by local authorities, year ending 31 March 2001. Department of Health.

1.17 Children in care/looked after in Scotland, by gender, 1988–2001

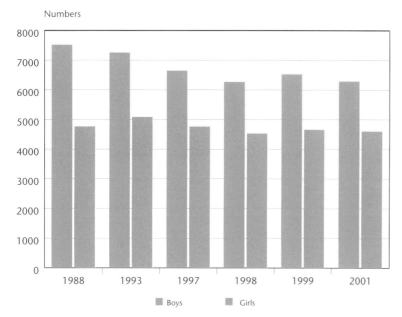

SOURCE: Scottish Executive National Statistics Publication 2002.

1.18 Children in care/looked after in Wales, by gender, 1980-2000

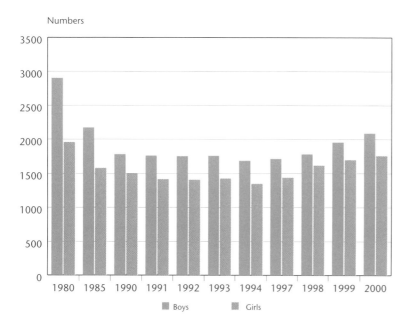

SOURCE: Social Services Statistics Wales 2001.

As far as gender is concerned figures in **Chart 1.16** show that boys have always outnumbered girls in this group, with the proportions for each gender remaining relatively stable across the years. Figures from Scotland and Wales are illustrated in **Charts 1.17 and 1.18**. It can be seen that the numbers are not rising in these two countries as they are in England.

The age distribution of children and young people being looked after in England in 2001 is set out in **Chart 1.19**. From this it can be seen that by far the greatest number are in the 10-15 age group. However, again this is based on a snapshot of the population, and masks the rapid throughput which is more heavily weighted towards younger children.

It is also of some interest to see how these placements are distributed among different types of care. Figures in **Chart 1.20** illustrate the placements for the adolescent population, showing that somewhere in the region of 20% are placed in residential care. A higher proportion is placed in foster care – among the 10-15 year-olds approximately two thirds receive this type of placement. In comparison with other ages teenagers are more likely to be placed in residential care, and if so they are more likely to be in secure units, homes and hostels rather than in other placements. However there seems to be little difference between age groups in the proportions living in foster families.

Finally in 2001 the Department of Health issued the first results of a survey of children in need in England. The definition of children in need stretches across a broader spectrum of difficulty than those looked after by local authorities. A break-down of the numbers involved is given in **Chart 1.21**, indicating that there are nearly four times as many children and young people remaining at home and receiving support from local authority agencies than there are those who are taken into care. This survey has shown that the main need for social service intervention is "abuse and neglect", which accounts for over half of all looked after children, and about one third of those remaining at home. Almost 12% of children in need are classified as disabled, and at least 16% are from ethnic minorities. While there may be some questions as to the definition of children in need, and in this case these are those in contact with social services, nonetheless the breakdown is helpful in giving some indication of the distribution of problems among the most vulnerable in our society.

1.19 Children and young people in care/looked after in England, by age, 2001

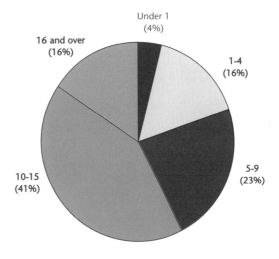

SOURCE: A/F 01/12: Children looked after by local authorities, year ending 31 March 2001. Department of Health.

1.20 Children and young people in care/looked after in England, by placement, 2001

			Numbers
Placement	All children	10-15	16 and over
Foster placements	38,400	16,600	4,600
Placed for adoption	3,400	210	-
Placement with parents	6,900	2,400	780
Other placements in the community	1,200	100	1,100
Secure units, homes and hostels	6,800	4,300	1,900
Other residential settings	680	240	270
Residential schools	1,100	750	280
All children	58,900	24,600	9,300

SOURCE: A/F 01/12: Children looked after by local authorities, year ending 31 March 2001. Department of Health.

1.21 Distribution of 'children in need' on a sample week: September/October 2001

Numbers and Percentages

England	Children Looked After		Children Supported in Families or Independently		Total Children in Need	
Type of need	Number	%	Number	%	Number	%
Abuse or neglect	33,700	54	41,100	26	74,900	34
Disability	7,000	11	20,200	13	27,200	12
Parental illness or disability	3,400	5	8,200	5	11,600	5
Family in acute distress	3,300	5	18,200	12	21,500	10
Family dysfunction	6,400	10	19,100	12	25,400	12
Socially unacceptable behaviour	2,000	3	10,700	7	12,700	6
Low income	200	0	10,700	7	10,900	5
Absent parenting	3,300	5	4,100	3	7,400	3
Cases other than CIN	500	1	5,900	4	6,400	3
Not stated	2,600	4	18,800	12	21,400	10
Total	**62,300**		**157,100**		**219,400**	

SOURCE: Children in Need in England: Preliminary results of a survey of activity and expenditure as reported by Local Authority Social Services' Children and Families Teams for a survey week in September/October 2001.

References

Berridge, D (2002) Child care. Research Matters. Community Care. London.

Bradshaw, J (Ed.) (2002) The well-being of children in the UK. Save the Children and University of York. York.

Haskey, J (2002) One parent families and the dependent children living with them in Great Britain. Population Trends. 109. 46-57.

Iacovou, M (2002) Regional differences in the transition to adulthood. Annals, AAPSS. 580. March. 40-69.

Iacovou, M and Berthoud, R (2001) Young people's lives: a map of Europe. Institute for Social and Economic Research. University of Essex. Colchester, Essex.

_____ (1999) Social focus on the family. The Stationery Office. London.

Chapter 2

Education, Training and Employment

2.1 Pupils having five or more GCSEs, grades A-C, by gender in England, 1980/81-2000/01

Percentages

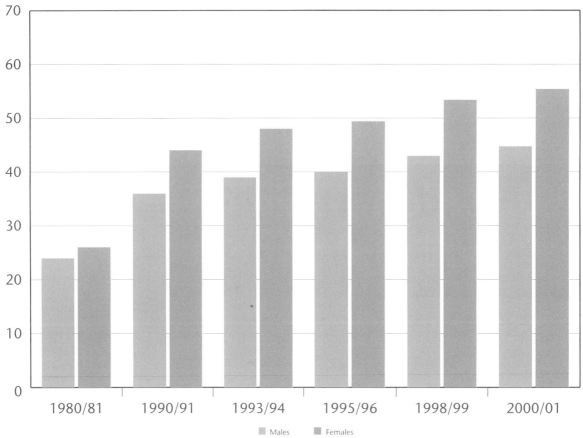

SOURCE: Regional Trends 37, 2002 edition. Office for National Statistics.

Education and Training

The world of education is undergoing substantial change at present. There are many reasons for this, some of which are to do with specific Government policies, whilst others are the result of wide-ranging social and economic change. Looking back over the last decade it is worth noting that the great majority of young people now remain in some form of education or training during the 16-18 year age period, and indeed many more continue into higher education. The further and higher education sectors have expanded rapidly to take account of increased demand, thus putting serious strain on the resources available within the sector. This expansion of student numbers relates also to the question of student funding. If more and more of those over the age of 16 remain in education or training, how can these young people be supported financially during late adolescence and early adulthood? Another issue of critical importance has to do with standards in schools, and the place of testing and examinations in the overall educational curriculum. In recent years much emphasis has been placed on improving standards in schools. This has led to increased use of league tables, and to a much greater emphasis being placed on examination results.

The first topic we will consider here is that of performance at GCSE. Figures in **Chart 2.1** show a marked increase in the number of pupils obtaining five or more

2.2 Pupils having five or more GCSEs, grades A-C, by gender in the four regions of the UK, 2000/01

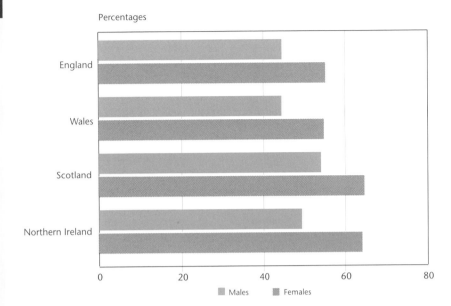

SOURCE: Regional Trends 37, 2002 edition. Office for National Statistics.

2.3 Pupils having five or more GCSEs, grades A-C, by regions of England, 2000/01

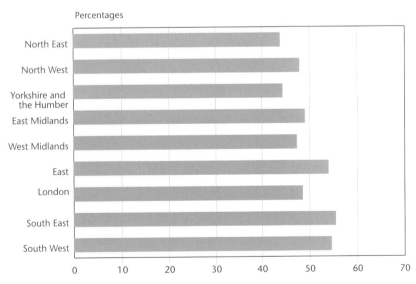

SOURCE: Regional Trends 37, 2002 edition. Office for National Statistics.

2.4 Pupils having five or more GCSEs, grades A-C, in England and Wales, by gender and ethnic origin, 2000

Percentages

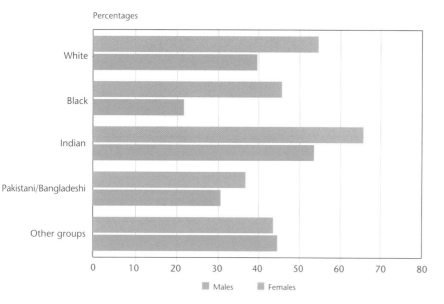

SOURCE: Social Trends 32: 2002 edition. Office for National Statistics.

2.5 Pupils having one or more GCE A-Level passes as a percentage of all in the 17-year age group, by gender in England, 1998/99-2000/01

Percentages

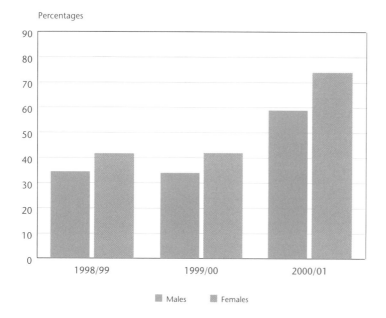

SOURCE: Statistical Bulletin May 2002. Department for Education and Skills.

GCSEs in the period 1990/91 to 2000/01. Over this period of ten years the number of young people in the UK obtaining five or more GCSEs at A-C grade has increased by roughly 10%. This is true for both boys and girls, although in an absolute sense girls substantially outperform boys at this level. The year-on-year improvement in the numbers of boys and girls achieving 5 or more passes at A-C grades clearly reflects the increased emphasis on the importance of examinations mentioned above. However, it should be underlined that there is a problem in separating out the effect of altered criteria for examination marking from genuinely better educational performance.

In **Chart 2.2** comparisons are drawn between the four countries of the UK, and it is evident that performance is better in Scotland and in Northern Ireland than it is in England and Wales. Figures in **Chart 2.3** illustrate regional variation within England, showing higher levels of achievement in the south of the country, and lower levels in the North-East and in Yorkshire and the Humber.

One key issue in looking at educational performance has to do with ethnicity, and as might be expected, there is marked variability in examination achievements between the different cultural groups in Britain. This is reflected in the data shown in **Chart 2.4**. From these figures it can be seen that Pakistani/Bangladeshi and Black pupils perform significantly less well than White or Indian pupils.

2.6 Pupils having one, two, three or more GCE A-Level passes as a percentage of all in the 17-year age group, by gender in England, 1998/99-2000/01

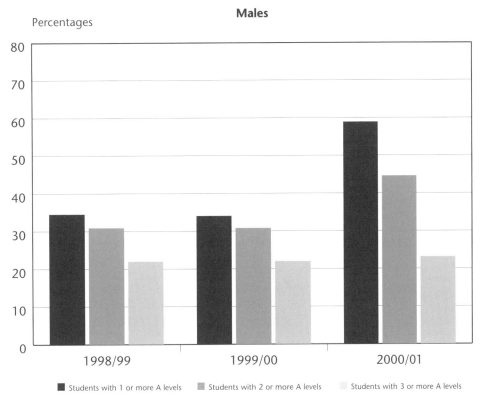

SOURCE: Statistical Bulletin May 2002. Department for Education and Skills.

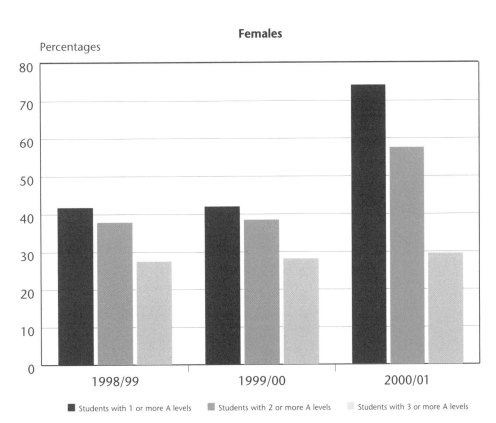

SOURCE: Statistical Bulletin May 2002. Department for Education and Skills.

2.7 Permanent exclusions from schools in England, 1994/95-2000/01

Numbers

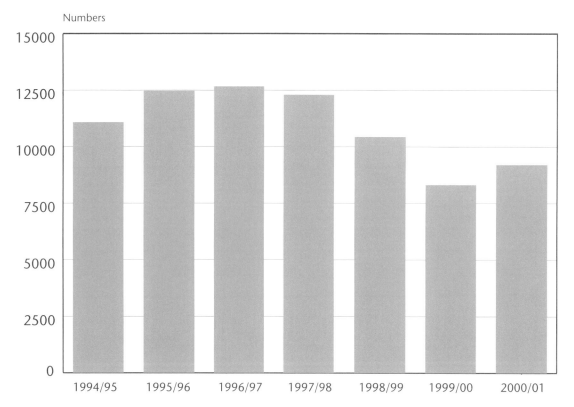

SOURCE: First Release. SFR 10/2002. Department for Education and Skills.

The gender differences are similar across groups, with girls doing better in every cultural group. The performance of Indian young people is in advance of all other groups, and especial note should be taken of Indian young women, 66% of whom achieve 5 or more passes at A-C grade at GCSE. This is the best performance by some way of any group of young people in the UK.

Turning now to A levels, figures in **Chart 2.5** indicate that the number achieving at least one A level pass over a three year period has increased from 34.5% to 58.9% of young men, and from 41.8% to 74.1% of young women as a percentage of the 17 year-old age group. This is a remarkable shift, and is indicative of a major and very recent change in the take-up of post-16 education. The increase in performance reflects the growing emphasis on educational attainments for this group of young people, as well as highlighting the demand for qualifications being expressed by employers. It also indicates a continuing trend towards better educational performance by females in comparison with their male colleagues.

In view of the importance of this trend, it is useful to look at figures showing other indices of A level performance. Figures in **Chart 2.6** show the number achieving one, two and three A levels. Here it can be seen that the marked increase in the number obtaining these examination passes is true of those with two A levels, but is not true of those with three A level passes. It is this latter group who are most

2.8 Proportions of exclusions in different schools, 2000/01

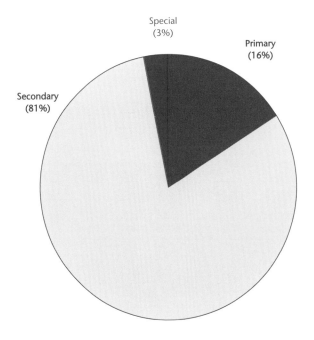

SOURCE: First Release. SFR 10/2002. Department for Education and Skills.

2.9 Permanent exclusions from schools in England by ethnic group, 2000/01

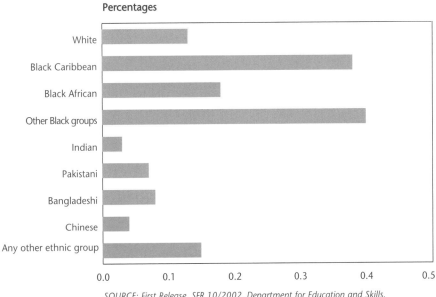

SOURCE: First Release. SFR 10/2002. Department for Education and Skills.

2.10 Student performance on a combined reading literacy scale, a mathematical literacy scale and a scientific literacy scale, by gender, for selected OECD countries, 2000

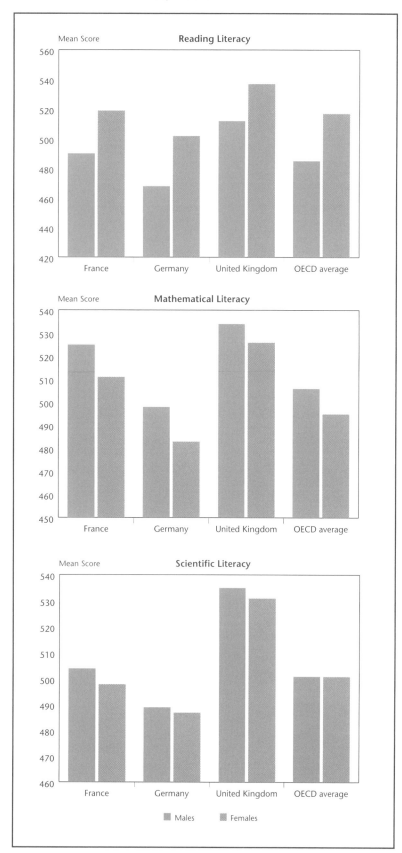

SOURCE: *Programme for International Student Assessment (PISA) 2000, OECD. www.pisa.oecd.org*

likely to be going on to higher education, and thus it would appear that the shift noted above applies most strongly to the group at the lower end of A level achievement.

A serious concern for all involved with secondary education has been the numbers of children and young people permanently excluded from school. In 1996/97 the number of those excluded reached over 12,000, and debate has continued as to how this group should be dealt with, and how best to offer them suitable education in a supportive environment. Figures in **Chart 2.7** indicate that the number of permanently excluded pupils has fallen since the high point in 1996/97, with the total falling into this category being 9,210 in 2000/01. The data in **Chart 2.8** show that of the total exclusions in 2000/01, 81% were from secondary school, whilst 16% were from primary school. Of all those excluded, 83% were male, a statistic which reflects the preponderance of boys involved in anti-social and challenging behaviour.

Another aspect of school exclusions is the high number of ethnic minority pupils who fall into this category. Figures in **Chart 2.9** show that while the exclusion rate for white pupils is 0.13%, the rate for Black Caribbean pupils, for example, is 0.38%. Admittedly this very high rate has fallen over the last decade, as attention has been paid to the problems of pupils from minority backgrounds. However, the rate for Black pupils in particular remains unacceptably high, and further work is needed to substantially reduce the level of permanent exclusions among this group.

Turning now to a very different feature of school performance, as a result of new research produced by the OECD, it has recently become possible to compare educational attainments among 15 year-olds in different countries. As part of the Programme for International Student Assessment (PISA), over a quarter of a million pupils in 32 countries were surveyed during the course of 2000. Performance in reading literacy, mathematical literacy and scientific literacy was measured, and a few of the results are set out in **Chart 2.10**. Results of this exercise are extremely interesting, and good news for British education when our achievements are compared with those of other European countries. In essence British pupils performed better in all areas than their European peers, with particularly good results in scientific literacy.

As was noted in the introduction to this chapter, a key change over the last fifteen years has been the increased numbers staying on in education post-16. A substantial shift is illustrated by the figures in **Chart 2.11**, which shows that there has been a sustained increase among this group since 1985. As will be noted, this trend is most marked for female students, with the percentage in this category rising from 55% to 76% over a span of 16 years.

2.11 Young people aged 16-18 in education and training in England, by gender, 1985-2001

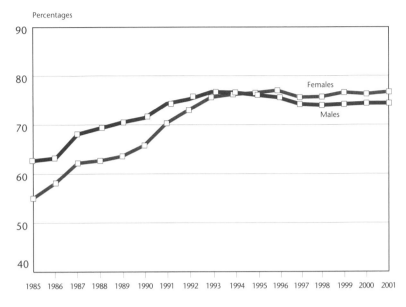

SOURCE: First Release. SFR 16/2002. Department for Education and Skills.

2.12 Total hours usually worked per week by Year 12 students as a percentage of all Year 12 students with jobs, in England and Wales, spring 2000

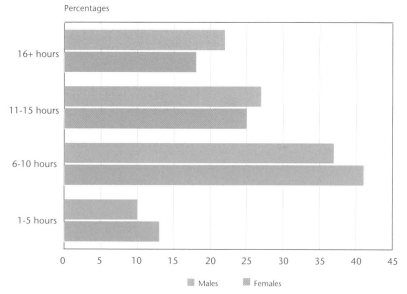

Percentages

SOURCE: Research Brief (RB323), 2001. Department for Education and Skills.

One of the worries relating to this group of students has to do with financial support. The Government has introduced a pilot scheme involving Educational Maintenance Alllowances (EMAs) for the poorest students, and early indications are that the scheme will be extended to reach a much wider group in due course. However, many students between the years of 16 and 18 are working part-time to fund their studies, and there is no doubt that part-time work does affect educational performance. Recent figures from Joan Payne of the Policy Studies Institute (2001) show that approximately 60% of pupils in Years 11 and 12 have had a part-time job at some time. As can be seen from **Chart 2.12**, of those who have had jobs roughly 40% work for 6-10 hours, whilst 20% work for more than 15 hours a week. More research is urgently needed with this group of students to assess the impact of combining work and study in this way.

Evidence from the OECD also makes it possible to compare the number of students engaged in education at age 18 in different European countries. As will be apparent from **Chart 2.13** Britain lags behind in this matter, with only 53% of 18 year-olds still in education. The differences between countries can partly be explained by the different school leaving ages in the various countries. Thus for example Germany has a school-leaving age of 18, whilst in Britain it is 16. Nonetheless the comparison is striking, and reflects important differences between ourselves and other European countries.

2.13 Participation in education at age 18 in different European countries, 1999

Percentages

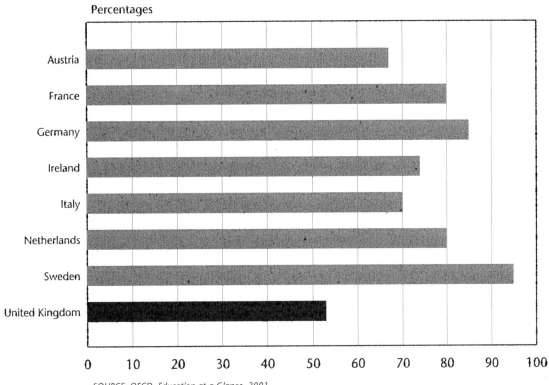

SOURCE: OECD, Education at a Glance, 2001.

2.14 Students in higher education in the UK, by gender, 1970/71 -2000/01

Thousands

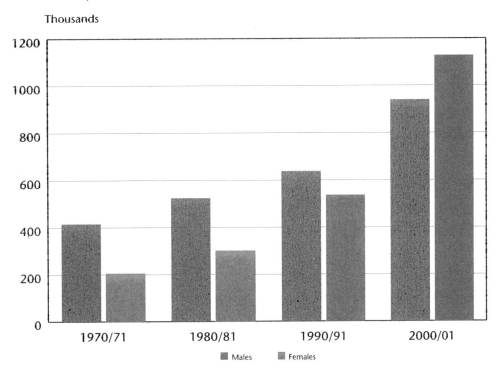

Males   Females

SOURCE: Social Trends 32: 2002 edition. Office for National Statistics.

2.15 Students in higher education, by type of course and gender, 2000/01

	Males	Females
		Thousands
Higher education		
Undergraduate		
Full time	511	602
Part time	228	320
Postgraduate		
Full time	82	81
Part time	118	124
All higher education	**940**	**1,128**

SOURCE: Social Trends 32: 2002 edition. Office for National Statistics.

We have already noted the trend towards increased participation in education and training for those over the age of 16. This trend is marked in further education, but even more marked when one looks at the picture in higher education. Figures illustrated in **Chart 2.14** show that the number of men in higher education in the UK has more than doubled between 1970/71 and 2000/01. However, the increase is even more stark for women, with a five-fold increase in this thirty year period. **Chart 2.15** shows the numbers and gender break-down of those in the different parts of the sector. Thus there are substantially more females than males in undergraduate education, while the numbers in postgraduate education are approximately equal.

Chart 2.16 illustrates the numbers in higher education coming from minority populations. As can be seen the group having the highest number in this sector is the Asian Indian group, followed by the Pakistani group. Most other minority groups have a much lower take-up of higher education in the UK, and it would be good to see some attempts made to increase these numbers in the future.

Finally in this section it is of interest to compare rates of involvement in tertiary education in Britain with those in other European countries. As can be seen from figures in **Chart 2.17** the UK has 22% engaged in education between the ages of 18 and 24, a rate which differs relatively little from other European countries. France is somewhat higher with 30% in tertiary education, whilst Germany is lower than the UK with only 15% in this sector.

2.16 Ethnic minority students in higher education, as a percentage of all applicants accepted through UCAS, in the UK, 2001/02

Percentages

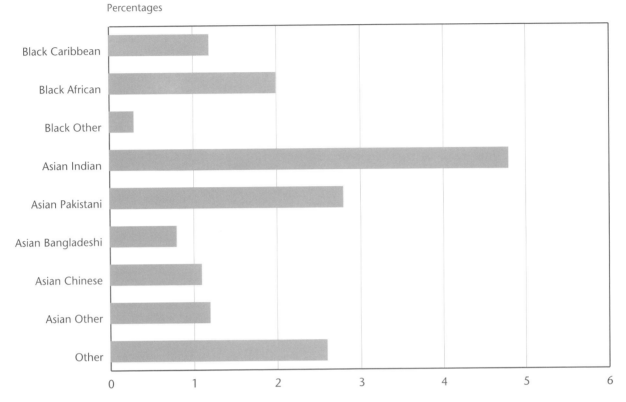

SOURCE: Trends in Education and Skills, DfES website.

2.17 Participation rates of 18-24 year-olds in tertiary education in selected EU countries, 1998/99

Percentages

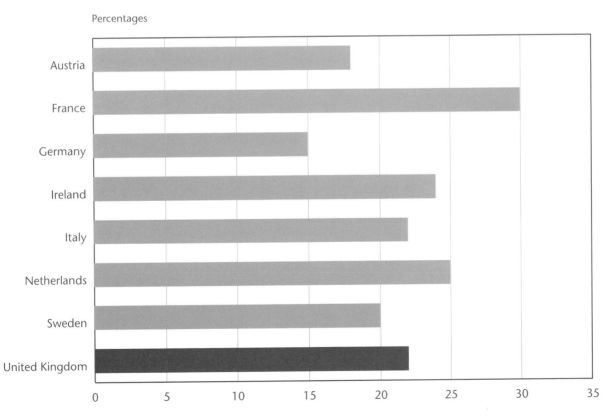

SOURCE: Eurostat Yearbook 2002: The Statistical Guide to Europe. Data 1990-2000.

2.18 Numbers of 16-24 year-olds in the labour force, in the UK, 1986-2001

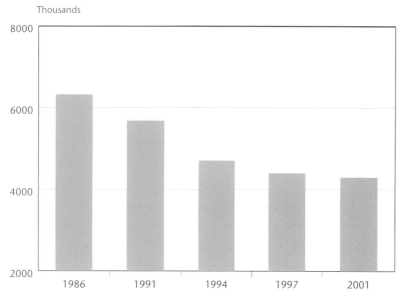

Thousands

SOURCE: Social Trends 26, 30 and 32. Office for National Statistics.

Employment

Changes in the labour market over the last twenty years have been profound, and these have had a substantial impact on young people. As we have seen in the previous section more and more young people remain in education and training after the statutory school leaving age, and entry into the labour market is thus delayed, often until the mid-twenties. One way to consider the issue is to look at the actual size of the workforce. Figures shown in **Chart 2.18** indicate that the number of 16-24 year-olds in the workforce in Britain has fallen by a significant margin since the middle of the 1980s. While to some extent this may be to due to a fall in the population amongst this age group, a greater contribution to the decrease is the shrinking of the job pool for all ages, and the vulnerability of younger workers in a time of reduced employment opportunities. We should also note the changed nature of the labour market, with a growth in service industry jobs, and a decline in manufacturing industry. These shifts create disadvantage for some groups of workers, and in such a situation young men who have low educational attainments are particularly at risk.

Another aspect of the employment picture has to do with unemployment. Figures in **Chart 2.19** indicate that rates of unemployment for those in the 18-24 age group have improved markedly over the last decade. The rate for young men has decreased from 19.0% in 1992 to 10.9% in

2.19 Unemployment rates in the UK, by age and gender, 1992-2001

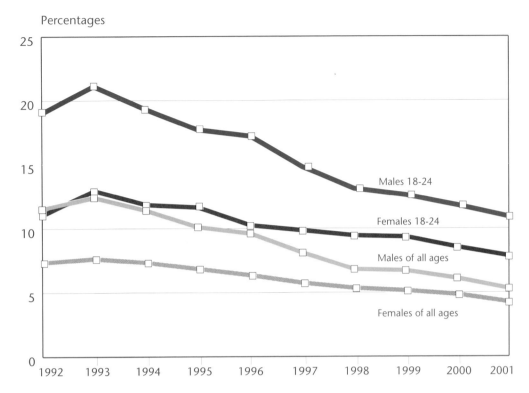

Percentages

SOURCE: Social Trends 32: 2002 edition. Office for National Statistics.

2.20 Unemployment rates for 16-24 year-olds by country and region in the UK, 2001-2002

Percentages

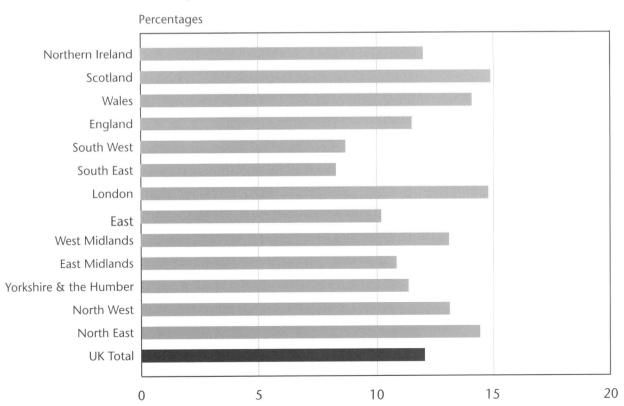

SOURCE: Regional Trends 37, 2002 edition. Office for National Statistics.

2.21 Unemployment rates for 16-24 year-olds, by ethnic group in the UK, 2000-01

Percentages

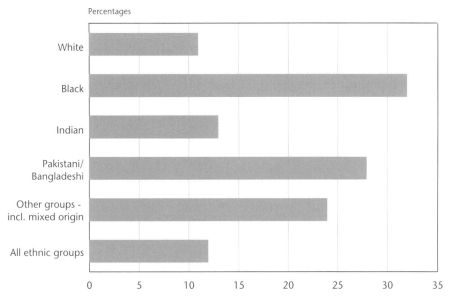

SOURCE: Social Trends 32: 2002 edition. Office for National Statistics.

2001, whilst the rate for young women has also decreased from 11.0% to 7.8%. It is not clear whether this change has to do with an increased take-up of education and training, or the introduction of the New Deal, or some combination of these factors. It is worth remarking that, in spite of the decreasing levels of unemployment among 18-24 year-olds, rates for this age group are still significantly higher than rates for any other age group in the population.

It should be noted that these figures are calculated by using the internationally accepted ILO definition of unemployment, namely those people who have sought work in the past four weeks, and are available to start work the following week. These are the figures currently used by the DfES, and it is upon these figures that the Labour Force Survey is based.

Turning now to regional trends, it can be seen from the figures in **Chart 2.20** that there is wide variation between different parts of the country in rates of unemployment. Rates are higher in Wales and Scotland than in England and Northern Ireland, and are higher also in London and the North-East than in other regions.

As far as unemployment and ethnicity are concerned, the situation is very worrying indeed, since there are extremely large differences between the white population and minority ethnic groups. The differences exist at all age levels, but are most striking for the 16-24 year age group. As can be seen in **Chart 2.21** rates are three times as high in the Black and Pakistani/Bangladeshi groups as they are in the white population.

Finally it is worth considering European comparisons of unemployment rates for those under 25 years of age, although such figures need to be treated with caution in view of the very different circumstances surrounding employment of young people in different countries. Figures in **Chart 2.22** indicate that Britain has lower rates than many countries, although there are some, such as Austria, Ireland and the Netherlands for example, where rates are significantly lower than those of the UK.

2.22 Unemployment rates for 15-24 year-olds in EU countries, 2000

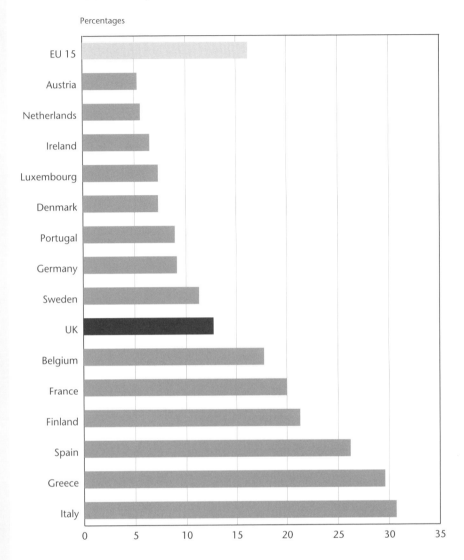

SOURCE: Eurostat Yearbook 2002: The Statistical Guide to Europe. Data 1990-2000.

References

Payne, J. (2001) Post - 16 students and part-time jobs: patterns and effect - a report based on the England and Wales Youth Cohort Study. Research Brief 323. December. Policy Studies Institute. London.

Chapter 3

Physical Health

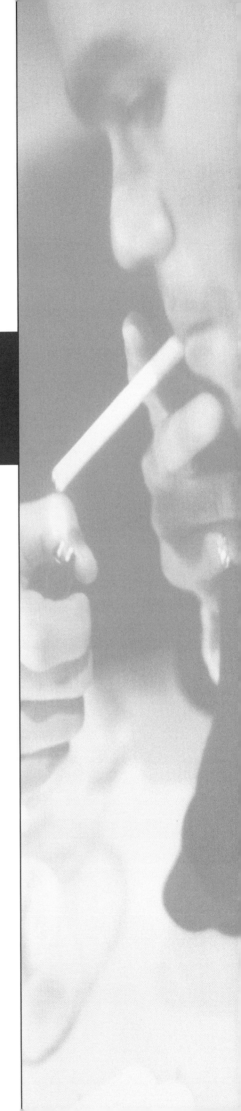

Physical Health

Over the past few years much greater attention has been paid to adolescent health than was the case in the past. This has been due to a number of factors, including a much greater recognition within Government departments of the importance of this area of specialty within broader areas of health policy. Over the past year much work has been carried out in relation to the establishment of the new National Service Framework, and it is hoped that when this is published in 2003 it will make possible far-reaching changes in the health care of children and young people in England and Wales. In addition to the impact of Government initiatives, recognition for their role in changing public perceptions should be paid to other public bodies, including many of the royal colleges, the Health Development Agency, and bodies established with a specific focus on one health area, such as drugs or alcohol.

Although it is generally accepted that adolescents are healthier than most other age groups, the last few years have seen a growing awareness that the picture is more complex than many realise. In the first place there are groups of young people whose health is problematic. Such groups include those growing up in poverty, as well as those in public care and in custody. Furthermore young people appear to have greater difficulty than other groups in accessing health provision, and attention has begun to focus on how to make services more accessible, and how to increase young people's participation in

3.1 Numbers of deaths in the UK, by age and gender, 2000

Numbers

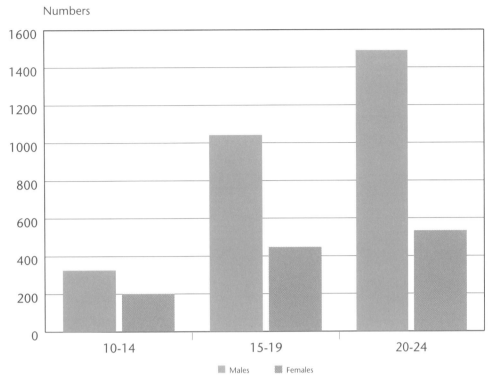

■ Males   ■ Females

SOURCE: Office for National Statistics, Mortality Statistics (series DH1 no. 33).

3.2 Reasons for consultation with a GP, over a twelve month period

Percentages

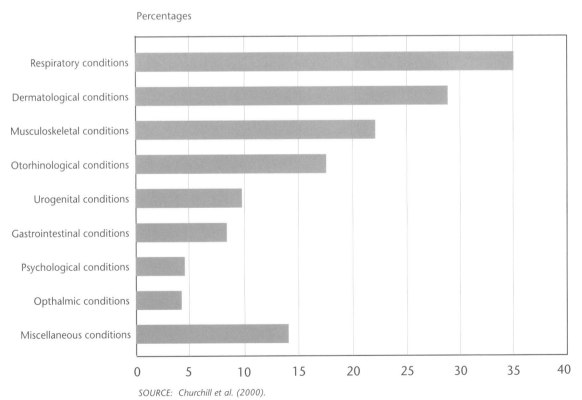

SOURCE: Churchill et al. (2000).

3.3 Aspects of primary care indentified as most important to young people

	Percentages
Confidentiality (knowing that if you tell the doctor something, other people will not find out)	81
Having a doctor who is interested in teenage problems	51
Being able to see a doctor on the same day you make the appointment	39
Having a special teenage clinic which you can 'drop into' if you have a problem	39
Being able to choose to see a male or female doctor	33
Being able to ask for advice over the phone without having to give your name	32
Having a friendly receptionist	30
Seeing the same doctor or nurse on every visit	20
Being able to discuss problems with a nurse instead of a doctor	17
Being invited to a special health check with a doctor or nurse	17

SOURCE: Churchill et al. (1997).

3.4 Consultations for different conditions among 15-16 year-olds, 1997

				Percentages	
Condition	No-one	GP	School nurse	Clinic	Other
Spots/acne	39.1	50.8	1.3	4.8	4.0
Diet	49.8	30.8	8.6	3.9	6.9
Smoking	63.5	16.0	8.7	3.4	8.3
Pregnancy	34.3	25.0	4.3	30.2	5.2
STDs	58.3	18.2	9.2	7.9	6.3

SOURCE: Jacobson et al. (2000).

service planning and delivery. One example of such work in this area is the rolling out of the National Healthy Schools Standard across the country. Such initiatives are welcome, and will be reflected in the information given below.

In this chapter we will firstly consider the rates of mortality in the adolescent age group. Apart from infancy, death rates among children and young people are highest in the 15-19 year age group, and are even higher in early adulthood. The change with age is primarily because deaths caused by injury and poisoning, as well as traffic accidents, increase developmentally. Figures in **Chart 3.1** show the overall numbers of deaths in 2000 in the United Kingdom. A clear gender difference is apparent, and this becomes more accentuated with age.

Turning now to morbidity, there have been some useful surveys of young people's health-related behaviour over the last decade in Britain. As far as reasons for consultations with the GP are concerned, a study by Churchill and colleagues (Churchill et al., 1997) reported on a sample of over 700 young people in the Midlands. They showed that 35% of all consultations were because of respiratory complaints, with other concerns such as skin complaints and sports injuries coming lower down the list. These figures are provided in **Chart 3.2**. Perhaps the most worrying aspect of these figures is the tiny number of teenagers who go to their GP with a mental health problem. We will be looking at this issue in more detail in Chapter 5.

Churchill and his colleagues also asked the young people in their sample what aspects of primary care were most important to them. Results in **Chart 3.3** show that confidentiality comes higher than any other factor, while being able to go to a doctor who has an interest in teenage problems comes next on the list.

In an interesting further study Jacobson et al. (2002) looked at the different consultation options used by young people for different health related concerns. From data in **Chart 3.4** it can be seen that teenagers are most likely to go to the GP for skin complaints, and least likely to go to the GP in respect of smoking or sexually transmitted infections. The school nurse is used relatively infrequently, whilst the clinic (usually understood to mean the family planning clinic) is used more often in relation to pregnancy. The aspect of these data which gives most concern is the very high numbers not using any source of advice from a health professional.

A somewhat different perspective on adolescent health is provided by the most recent Health Education Authority (now the Health Development Agency) survey involving over 10,000 young people between the ages of 11 and 16 (Haselden et al., 1999). In this study young people were asked about symptoms they experienced at least once a week. Figures are provided in **Chart 3.5** showing, as might be expected, that headaches and emotional distress of various sorts are the most common symptoms of ill-health in this group. In terms of gender, females suffer more headaches and stomachaches than males.

3.5 Symptoms experienced at least once a week by young people 11-15 years of age, by gender, in England, 1997

		Percentages
	Males	Females
Headache	23	35
Stomachache	15	23
Backache	13	14
Feeling low	23	31
Irritability or bad temper	42	43
Feeling nervous or anxious	28	34
Difficulties in getting to sleep	29	33
Feeling dizzy	15	17

SOURCE: Haselden, Angle and Hickman (1999).

3.6 Complaints for which remedies have been taken in the last week by 12-15 year-olds, by gender

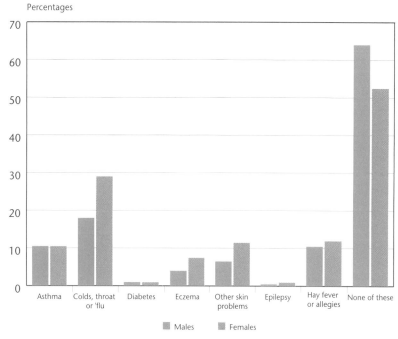

Percentages

SOURCE: Balding (2002).

The question of symptomatology was also asked by Balding in his annual survey (Balding, 2002), and figures in **Chart 3.6** reflect complaints for which some remedy has been taken during the last week prior to the administration of the questionnaire. Most common here are colds and flu, followed by allergies, eczema and other skin complaints. There is a small gender difference, but not as large as the one found in the Haselden et al. survey.

There has been a continuing interest in the use made by young people of primary health care services. Kari et al. (1997) studied a sample of over 4,000 young people aged 15 and 16, and reported that the median number of consultations in this group was 2 per year for young men and 3 per year for young women. Others, such as Saxena et al. (1999), have found much the same level of attendance among 10 to 15 year-olds. In the most recent Balding survey, results concerning GP consultations are reported in a somewhat different manner. As can be seen in **Chart 3.7** the sample is divided into those attending very recently, at various points over the previous year, and then more than a year ago. Looking at the data in this manner indicates that fewer than 15% of young people have not gone to the doctor at all within a one-year period.

This question has also been considered in respect of the older age group, those between the ages of 16 and 19. In a survey carried out by the Exeter Schools Health Education Unit in 2002, the researchers asked a sample of nearly 1,000 students attending FE colleges

3.7 Frequency of visiting the doctor among 12-15 year olds, by gender, 2001

Percentages

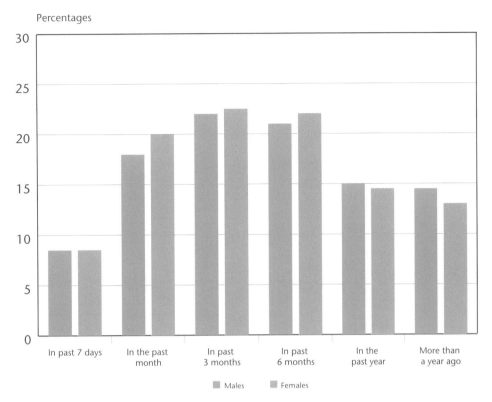

Males   Females

SOURCE: Balding (2002).

3.8 Frequency of visiting the doctor among 16-19 year-olds, by gender, 2002

Percentages

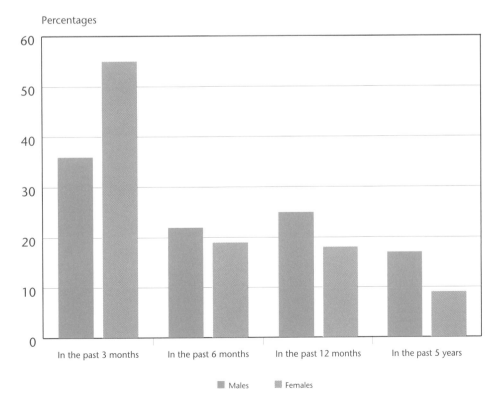

Males   Females

SOURCE: Further Education Student Health and Lifestyle Survey, 2002. Schools Health Education Unit.

3.9 Main reason for seeing the doctor at last visit among 16-19 year-olds, by gender, 2002

Percentages

	Male	Female
Coughs, colds, flu, ear infections	31	19
Skin problems	12	12
Cervical smear test	0	2
Contraception	1	19
Immunisation (vaccination)	4	1
Blood test	4	7
Allergies (inc hay fever)	0	4
Asthma	5	3
Depression, worry, anxiety (or other emotional problems)	4	4
Headache, migraine	3	4
Pregnancy or suspected pregnancy	0	3
Sexually transmitted infection	1	2
Muscular-skeletal problems	8	7
Gastric problems	0	2
Injury	9	4
Cannot remember	6	4
Other	10	6

SOURCE: Further Education Student Health and Lifestyle Survey, 2002. Schools Health Education Unit.

3.10 Dieting to lose weight, by gender and school year, in England, 1997

Percentages

	School Year				
	7	8	9	10	11
Males					
Yes I am dieting to lose weight	6	5	5	7	3
No, but should lose weight	18	19	19	15	16
No, because my weight is fine	74	74	75	78	78
Not stated	2	2	1	2	2
Base (100%)	1073	1011	1051	1009	917
Females					
Yes I am dieting to lose weight	9	13	13	19	17
No, but should lose weight	22	26	26	30	30
No, because my weight is fine	68	60	59	50	52
Not stated	1	1	1	1	1
Base (100%)	1102	1040	1042	1087	967

SOURCE: Haselden, Angle and Hickman (1999).

about their attendance at the GP. Results can be seen in **Chart 3.8**, and it may be noted that by far the greatest majority attend within one year, only 9% of young women and 17% of young men not attending during the course of a year. Also of interest is the fact that a much higher proportion of young women than young men attend within a three-month period. Reasons given for attending the doctor among this sample are given in **Chart 3.9**, differing in some important respects from the reasons given by the younger age group seen in **Chart 3.2**.

Turning now to food intake and dieting, a topic of concern not only to parents but to public health specialists as well, recent studies have been helpful in providing a fuller picture than had been previously available. As far as dieting is concerned, figures reported in the Haselden et al. (1999) study mentioned earlier indicate that the numbers involved in this behaviour are perhaps not as large as the public would expect. Some of these data are illustrated in **Chart 3.10**. This shows that the greatest number are dieting in Year 10, where 19% of females and 4% of males report this behaviour. In addition 30% of girls and 15% of boys at this age indicate that they believe their weight is too high.

Adolescent health, especially physical health, is very much affected by the degree of risk behaviour engaged in by young people. Three major areas of concern here are smoking, drinking and the use of illegal drugs. Large amounts of data are available in all

3.11 Proportion of young people who are current smokers, by school year and gender, in England, 1997

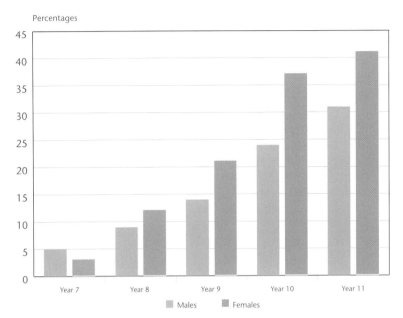

SOURCE: Haselden, Angle and Hickman (1999).

3.12 Proportion of pupils who were regular smokers among 15-16 year-olds, by gender, 1982-2001

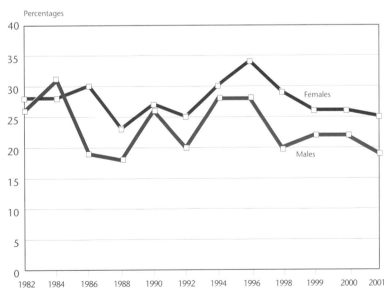

SOURCE: Boreham and Shaw (2001), Boreham and Shaw (2002).

3.13 Smoking behaviour among 15 year-olds, by gender, 2001

	Percentages
Boys	
Regular smoker	19
Occasional smoker	10
Used to smoke	12
Current or ex-smoker	41
Tried smoking	21
Never smoked	38
Tried once or never smoked	59
Girls	
Regular smoker	25
Occasional smoker	15
Used to smoke	12
Current or ex-smoker	52
Tried smoking	19
Never smoked	29
Tried once or never smoked	48

SOURCE: Boreham and Shaw (2002).

3.14 Proportion of 16-19 year-olds smoking in Britain, by gender, 1974-2001

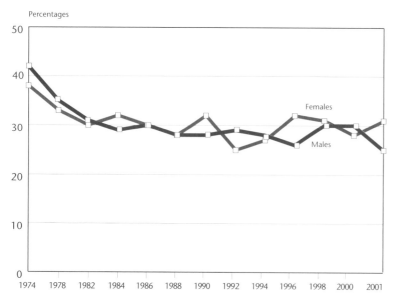

SOURCE: Living in Britain, results from the 2001 General Household Survey. The Stationery Office, 2002.

these areas, although studies are not always comparable because of the different methods used. Turning first to smoking, it will be apparent from **Chart 3.11** that smoking rates increase markedly throughout the secondary school age range, with a clear gender difference at all ages. These figures are again taken from the study by Haselden et al. (1999).

Considering this issue from a historical perspective, it can be seen from **Chart 3.12** that the percentages of those who were regular smokers among 15-16 year-olds have not varied greatly over a 19-year time span. There appeared to be an increase in the 1990s, but the levels of smoking have now dropped, and are similar to those seen in the 1980s. Again it can be seen that girls are more likely to be regular smokers than boys. If one looks at smoking behaviour in more detail the gender difference is maintained. As can be seen in **Chart 3.13** among 15 year-olds there are more boys than girls who have never smoked, and among occasional smokers there are more girls than boys.

In contrast to the secondary school age group, there is some evidence that levels of smoking among older groups have declined. Figures in **Charts 3.14** and **3.15** illustrate the historical trends for 16-19 year-olds and 20-24 year-olds. From these data it can be seen that smoking has diminished since 1974, although the trend is more marked in the earlier half of the time period than in more recent years. Finally it can be seen from **Chart 3.16** that there are no major differences between most European countries in smoking rates among young people.

In respect of the differences that do exist the countries of Great Britain fall somewhere in the mid-range for smoking behaviour.

We will now look at drinking, a different type of risk behaviour for young people. We will firstly consider the percentages of young people between the ages of 11 and 15 who drank alcohol in the last week. Figures in **Chart 3.17** indicate that, as expected, alcohol use increases with age, and that boys are marginally more likely to be drinking than girls. By age 15, 52% of boys and 46% of girls report that they drank alcohol in the last week.

Looking at this age group as a whole, and considering the mean number of units of alcohol drunk over a one-week period, it can be seen from **Chart 3.18** that there has been a dramatic increase in the amount of alcohol being consumed among teenagers. It is apparent that alcohol consumption by those in this age group has more than doubled in the ten-year period from 1990 to 2000. A similar although not quite so marked increase in alcohol use among the older group of 16-24 year-olds has also taken place in roughly the same time span, and is illustrated in **Chart 3.19**.

A cross-European comparison of alcohol-related behaviour underlines just how worrying these trends are. As can be seen from **Chart 3.20** England, Scotland, Wales and Northern Ireland have some of the highest levels of alcohol use among young people in the European Union, similar only to Denmark. Such figures raise major problems for health educators and policy makers, not to mention parents and

3.15 Proportion of 20-24 year-olds smoking in Britain, by gender, 1974-2001

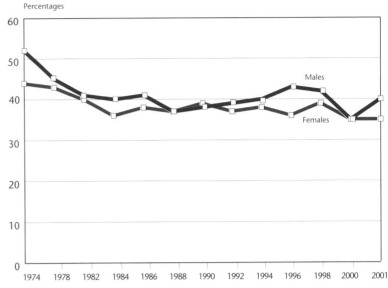

SOURCE: *Living in Britain, results from the 2001 General Household Survey. The Stationery Office, 2002.*

3.16 Proportion of 15 year-olds who report smoking at least weekly, in selected countries, 1997/98

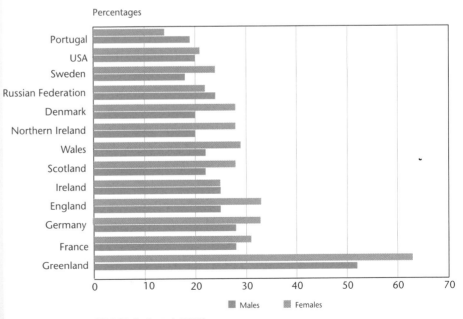

SOURCE: *Currie et al. (2000).*

3.17 Percentage of pupils who drank alcohol last week, by gender and age, 2000

Percentages

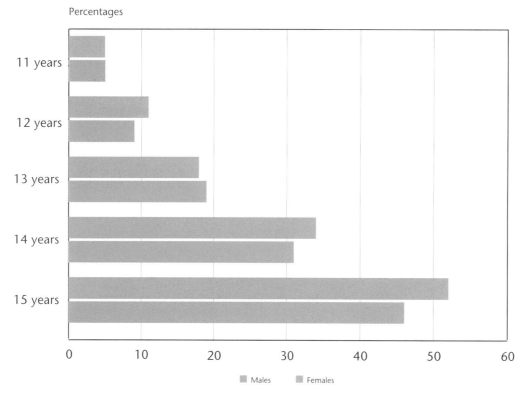

SOURCE: Boreham and Shaw (2001).

3.18 Mean units of alcohol consumed in last 7 days, among 11-15 year-olds in England, by gender, 1990-2000

Units

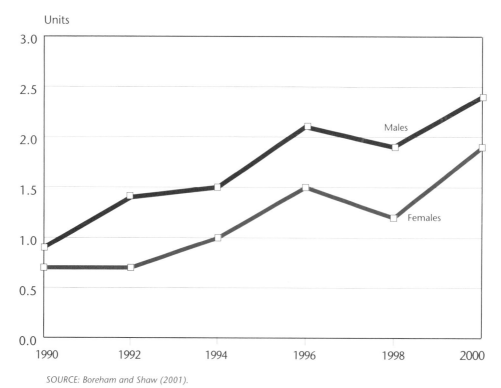

SOURCE: Boreham and Shaw (2001).

3.19 Mean units of alcohol consumed in last 7 days, among 16-24 year-olds in the UK, by gender, 1992-2001

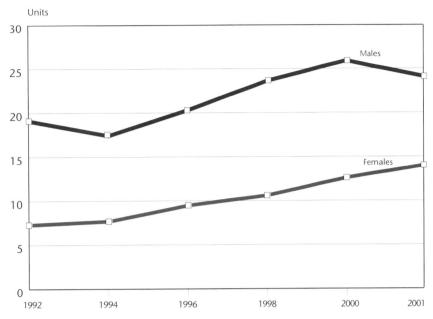

SOURCE: Living in Britain, results from the 2001 General Household Survey. The Stationery Office, 2002.

3.20 Proportion of 15 year-olds who report drinking beer, wine or spirits at least weekly, in selected countries, 1997/98

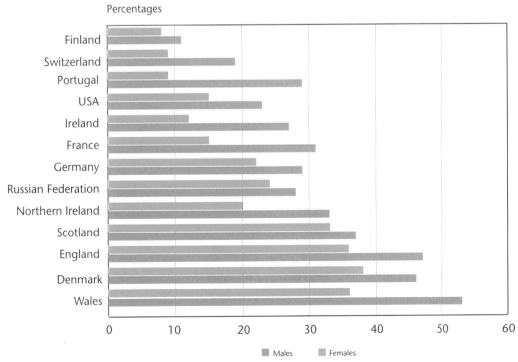

SOURCE: Currie et al. (2000).

3.21 Proportion of 15-16 year-olds who reported 'binge drinking' 3 times or more during the last 30 days, by gender, in selected countries, 1999

Percentages

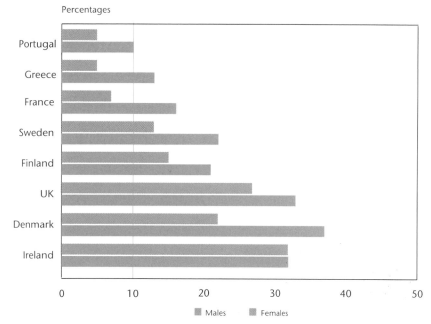

Males ■ Females ■

SOURCE: The 1999 European School Survey Project on Alcohol and Other Drugs Report, 2000.

3.22 Proportions who used cannabis or any Class A drug in 2001, by age

Percentages

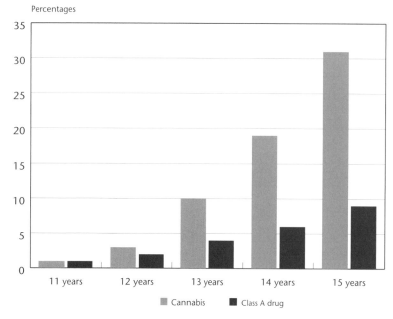

Cannabis ■ Class A drug ■

SOURCE: Boreham and Shaw (2002).

carers of young people. Evidence on binge drinking further underlines the same point, with data illustrated in **Chart 3.21** again placing the UK in a worse position than most other European countries with respect to this behaviour.

We now turn to the subject of illegal drug use among young people. Readers will be aware that over the last two years there has been much debate about the status of cannabis as an illegal drug. In July 2002 the Home Secretary announced plans to reclassify cannabis from a Class B to a Class C drug. Such a proposal does not go as far as many had hoped, but if passed into law in 2003, it will clearly have an impact both on public attitudes to the drug as well as on the behaviour of young people and law enforcement agencies. In respect of data reported here, however, we will be still be discussing a situation in which cannabis is classified as a Class B drug in the same category as amphetamines and barbiturates.

As might be expected, there is a substantial amount of data available on illegal drug use among adolescents, although not all of the findings are consistent. Different methods and varying samples inevitably lead to differing results. One of the most reputable series of studies is that carried out by those working for the Office for National Statistics. In the most recent study (Boreham and Shaw, 2002), the changes with age between 11 and 15 are charted both in respect of cannabis use as well as the use of Class A drugs (heroin, cocaine, ecstasy and similar substances). These data are illustrated in **Chart 3.22**, and show that, by the age of 15, 31% have used cannabis whilst 9% have used a Class A drug. Another study which provides corroborative evidence of these trends is the one carried out by Balding in Exeter (Balding, 2002). Findings from this survey are illustrated in **Chart 3.23**, indicating that in this sample slightly less than 30% have used cannabis by age 15.

As far as the older age group is concerned, a useful study by Howard Parker and colleagues (Parker et al., 2002) reports on a long-term follow up of illegal drug use among a large sample in the North-West of England. These young people have been followed from age 14 to age 22, and some of the findings from this study are illustrated in **Chart 3.24**. Here it can be seen that cannabis use increases from 17.7% to 31.6% across this age range, whilst the use of ecstasy increases from 2.6% to 7.8%. Interestingly the use of solvents decreases with age, as does the use of magic mushrooms.

Turning now to European comparisons, figures in **Chart 3.25** show that the UK has higher rates of illegal drug use among young people than most other similar countries apart from France. Thus in respect of both drinking and illegal drug use young people in England, Scotland, Wales and Northern Ireland would appear to be more involved in risk behaviour than their counterparts across Europe. Such findings raise serious questions which need urgently to be addressed by both policy-makers as well as those in health education. However we may note one encouraging piece of evidence,

3.23 Proportion of pupils who have used cannabis, ecstasy or solvents, by school year and gender, 2001

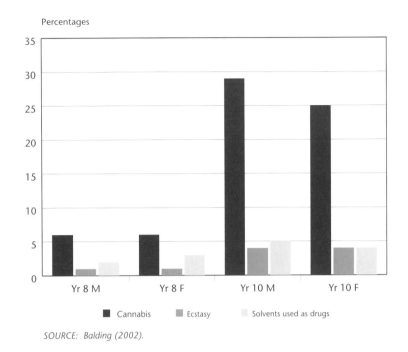

SOURCE: Balding (2002).

3.24 Past year prevalence of illicit drug taking (age 14-22 years) by individual drug, 2000

Percentages

	14 yrs	15 yrs	16 yrs	17 yrs	18 yrs	20 yrs	22 yrs
Amphetamines	4.1	6.8	8.8	16.6	24.0	20.9	11.0
Amyl nitrites	5.3	9.8	10.3	17.4	20.4	17.2	10.3
Cannabis	9.2	12.3	11.3	44.0	47.8	47.3	46.8
Cocaine powder	0.4	1.5	1.1	2.6	4.0	8.2	16.2
Crack cocaine	-	-	-	0.0	0.4	0.6	0.9
Ecstasy	2.3	2.7	1.9	9.5	17.4	15.1	14.5
Heroin	0.2	0.8	0.6	0.4	0.2	0.2	0.2
LSD	6.3	8.7	9.4	13.2	15.2	10.3	2.8
Magic mushrooms	3.2	4.8	4.2	4.0	4.2	4.2	1.7
Solvents	4.1	4.0	1.5	2.2	1.1	0.5	0.0
Tranquillisers	0.7	2.3	0.8	1.9	1.5	1.9	1.1
At least one drug	30.9	40.6	40.5	46.1	52.9	58.2	52.1

SOURCE: Parker, Williams and Aldridge (2002).

3.25 Proportion of 15-16 year-olds who have used marijuana or hashish during the last 30 days, in selected countries, by gender, 1999

Percentages

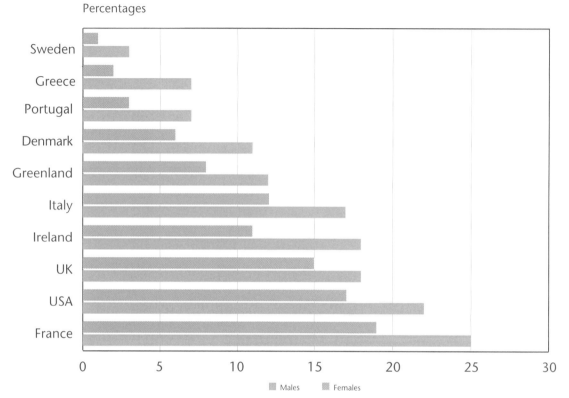

SOURCE: *The 1999 European School Survey Project on Alcohol and Other Drugs Report, 2000.*

3.26 Proportion of pupils who remembered receiving health education on various topics in last year, 1988-2000

Percentages

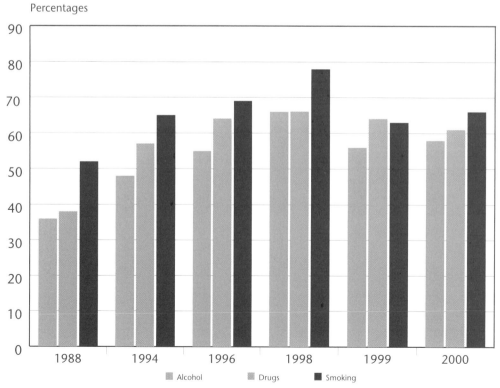

SOURCE: *Boreham and Shaw (2001).*

recorded in the study by Boreham and Shaw (2001) of smoking, drinking and drug use. These authors asked young people in their sample how many of them remembered receiving health education on the various topic areas, and then compared these findings with similar findings from previous studies. As can be seen from **Chart 3.26**, there is some evidence that there has been an increase in the numbers of those remembering having received health education between the years of 1988 and 2000, particularly in respect of alcohol and drugs education.

The last topic to be considered in this chapter is that of physical exercise. In the public mind there is continuing concern about the perceived decrease in physical activity among young people, and we now look at some evidence on this question. Figures from the most recent study of exercise among 11 to 15 year-olds are shown in **Chart 3.27**. These indicate that boys at all ages are more likely to be involved in physical activity, with the gap between the genders becoming more pronounced with age. Looking at those in Year 11 (15 year-olds) it can be seen that only 20% of boys take exercise once a week or less, whilst 49% of girls fall into this category.

Another way of looking at these data is to consider how frequently young people take vigorous exercise over a period of one week. As can be seen from **Chart 3.28** only 15% of girls and 12% of boys take no exercise, whilst 45% of boys and 30% of girls take exercise three days or more in the week. Finally, an interesting historical comparison can

3.27 Occasions of physical activity undertaken outside school hours, by gender and school year, in England, 1997

Percentages

		School Year				
	Total	7	8	9	10	11
Males						
Every day	29	30	31	30	32	24
4-6 times a week	25	24	25	2	23	26
2-3 times a week	25	23	25	25	24	29
Once a week	12	13	11	13	13	13
Once a month	2	2	2	2	2	3
Less than once a month	2	2	2	2	3	2
Never	3	5	3	2	3	2
Not stated	1	1	1	<0.5	1	1
Base (=100%)	5063	1073	1011	1051	1009	917
Females						
Every day	15	21	18	15	12	10
4-6 times a week	16	22	20	17	1	10
2-3 times a week	30	28	31	31	29	29
Once a week	23	18	20	23	27	28
Once a month	5	3	4	6	7	8
Less than once a month	5	4	3	4	6	7
Never	5	4	4	4	5	6
Not stated	<0.5	1	<0.5	<0.5	<0.5	1
Base (=100%)	5241	1105	1040	1042	1087	967

SOURCE: *Haselden, Angle and Hickman (1999).*

3.28 Number of days in which vigorous exercise was taken during the last week among 10-15 year-olds, by gender, in England, 2001

Percentages

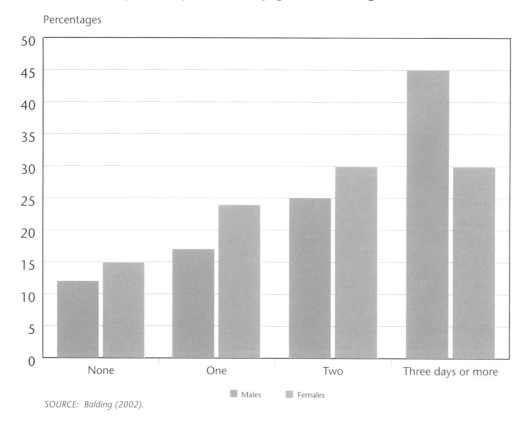

SOURCE: Balding (2002).

3.29 Proportion of girls aged 14-15 years-old who do not participate in any active sports on a weekly basis, 1992-2001

Percentages

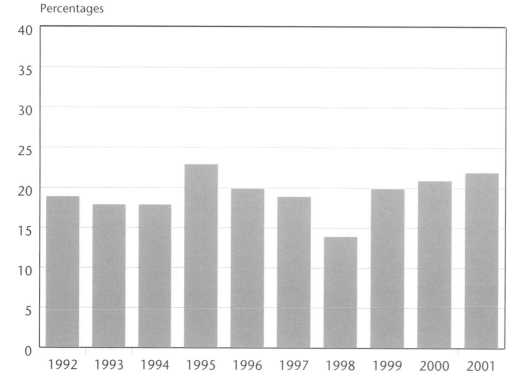

SOURCE: Balding (2002).

be drawn by looking at the figures illustrated in **Chart 3.29**. Balding has considered the numbers of 14 and 15 year-old girls who do not participate in any exercise. Contrasting figures in 1992 with those in 2001 it can be seen that, at the very least, there has been no substantial increase in the proportions falling into this unfortunate category during the 1990s.

References

Balding, J (2002) Young people in 2001. Schools Health Education Unit. Exeter.

Boreham, R and Shaw, A (2001) Smoking, drinking and drug use among young people in England in 2000. The Stationery Office. London.

Boreham, R and Shaw, A (2002) Drug use, smoking and drinking among young people in England in 2001. The Stationery Office. London.

Churchill, R et al. (1997) Factors influencing the use of general practice-based health services by teenagers. Division of General Practice, University of Nottingham. Nottingham.

Churchill, R et al. (2000) Do the attitudes and beliefs of young teenagers towards general practice influence actual consultation behaviour? British Journal of General Practice. 50. 953-957.

Currie, C et al. (Eds) (2000) Health and health behaviour among young people. World Health Organisation. Denmark.

Haselden, L, Angle, H and Hickman, M (1999) Young people and health: health behaviour in school-aged children. Health Education Authority. London.

Hibell, B et al. (2000) The 1999 European school survey project on alcohol and other drugs report. The Swedish Council for Information on Alcohol and Other Drugs (CAN), The Pompidou Group at the Council of Europe. Sweden.

Jacobson, L et al. (2000) Teenagers' views on general practice consultations and other medical advice. Family Practice. 17. 156-158.

Kari, J et al. (1997) Adolescents' attitudes to general practice in North London. British Journal of General Practice. 47. 109-111.

Parker, H, Williams, L and Aldridge, J (2002) The normalisation of 'sensible' recreational drug use: further evidence from the North West England longitudinal study. Sociology. 36(4). 941-964.

Saxena, S, Majeed, A and Jones, M (1999) Socio-economic differences in childhood consultation rates in general practice in England and Wales. British Medical Journal. 318. 642-647.

Chapter 4

Sexual Health

Sexual Health

The sexual health of young people is a matter of intense public concern, as well as being a major issue for parents and carers. In recent years there has been much publicity given to the fact that Britain has the highest rate of teenage pregnancy among European countries. In response to this situation the Government has established the Teenage Pregnancy Unit in the Department of Health, and has set clear targets for the reduction of rates of teenage pregnancy over the next five and ten year periods. In addition new guidance on the teaching of sex and relationships education (SRE) has been issued by the DfES. The Teenage Pregnancy Unit has put in place an extensive programme aimed at reducing rates of teenage pregnancy, particularly among those under the age of 16, and in comparison with only a few years ago there is today a much greater sense of purpose among health professionals, as well as closer collaboration between agencies. It is still too early to tell how these measures will affect rates of teenage pregnancy in the long-term, but there are encouraging signs at present, with conception rates among both the under-16s and the under-20s showing a continuing downward trend since the establishment of the Unit.

As far as research evidence on the sexual behaviour of young people is concerned, it is still the case that there are very few empirical studies that have been carried out in the UK. In the last few years there have been two exceptions to this, and we will turn now to look at the findings from these studies. First, Marion Henderson, Daniel Wight and colleagues have carried out a detailed survey of a large sample of 14 year-olds in Scotland (Wight and Henderson, 2000; Henderson et al., 2002). This is a very unusual study, the first of its kind in Britain, and it enables us to get a sense of the range of sexual activity among this age group. Figures in **Chart 4.1** show that 18% of boys and 15% of girls report having had full sexual intercourse, whilst between a third and a half of the sample have engaged in heavy petting. These authors also provide evidence on the frequency of sexual intercourse, reporting that a third of the sample have only had sex once, and a further 52% have had only one sexual partner.

The second recent study to note is that of Wellings et al. (2001), which continues the work of the National Survey of Sexual Attitudes and Lifestyles (NATSAL). An earlier survey along similar lines was reported eight years ago (Johnson et al., 1994). Figures in **Chart 4.2** make it possible to compare sexual behaviour at different time points since the 1960s. All four studies have data on the number of 16-19 year-olds reporting that they had had sex before the age of 16. It has to be recognized that the methodology is not the same in all studies, and the size of the samples varies widely. Nonetheless a comparison of this sort does give an indication of the historical changes in sexual behaviour seen over the last 40 years.

4.1 Range of sexual activity among 14 year-olds in Scotland

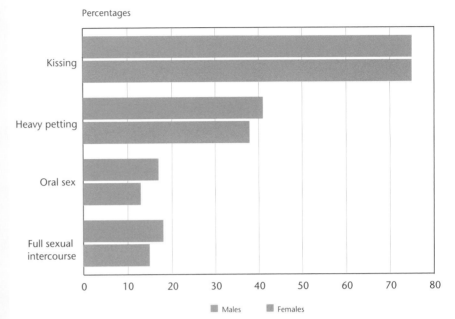

SOURCE: Wight and Henderson (2000); Henderson et al. (2002).

4.2 First sexual intercourse before the age of 16 by gender

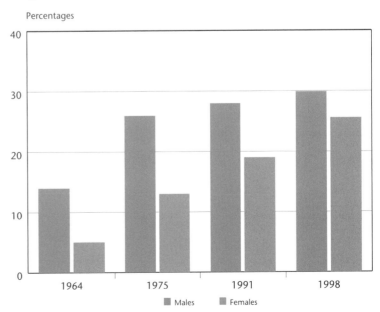

SOURCE: Schofield (1965); Farrell (1978); Johnson et al. (1994) and Wellings et al. (2001).

4.3 Conception rates in England and Wales, 13-15 year-olds, 1969-2000

Rate per 1,000 females

SOURCE: Population Trends. Spring 2002. Office for National Statistics.

In essence the number reporting having had sex before the age of 16 has risen slowly over this period, with the least change having taken place in the 1990s. The disparity between the genders has gradually diminished, the figures for males and females being closest in 1998. One possibility here is that as equality between the genders has increased, women have gained confidence in relation to their sexual behaviour, and have felt more able to report it freely. An alternative explanation is that in the past men have generally over-reported their sexual activity. It may well be that a combination of these factors has been at work, but even so it does not disguise the fact that more young people under the age of 16 have become sexually active over the last decades.

It is instructive now to turn to conception rates among young women. As we have noted there has been much public and political concern over Britain's position in the European league table for teenage pregnancy, and much effort has been invested in developing means to reduce the rates in the UK. Evidence presented in **Chart 4.3** indicates that the conception rate for those under 16 has fallen from 9.3 per thousand in 1991 to 8.3 per thousand in 2000. Furthermore data released by the Teenage Pregnancy Unit indicate that, considering quarterly rates in 2001, there would appear to be a continuing fall on this measure. This is encouraging, and points to the possibility that the work of the Teenage Pregnancy Unit is having an impact already. However, as can also be seen from this Chart, the rate in 1993 was even lower than in 2000, at 8.1 per thousand. Thus we can only conclude that we are still some way from being able to confirm a genuinely sustained and long-term decrease in rates of conceptions among the under-16s.

Rates for Scotland are shown in **Chart 4.4**. These show much the same pattern and variability as in England and Wales. While comparisons between Scotland, England and Wales may not reveal major differences, there is of course substantial regional variation in conception rates. Broadly speaking rates are lower in areas that are more affluent, and higher in areas of greater deprivation. Something of the variation can be seen in the fact that, in 2000, Lambeth, Southwark and Lewisham Health Authority – an inner London borough – had a conception rate of 114.1 per thousand women aged 15-19, whilst in East and West Surrey, the rate was 37.1 per thousand women. (Brook Advisory Centre Factsheet 2: Teenage Conceptions - Statistics and Trends, April 2002).

As far as the outcome of pregnancy is concerned, it can be seen from **Chart 4.5** that conceptions leading to maternity among 13-15 year-olds have decreased since 1969, while the number of abortions in this age group has increased correspondingly. The main change occurred in the early 1970s, following the introduction of the 1967 Abortion Act.

4.4 Conception rates in Scotland, 13-15 year-olds, 1983-2000

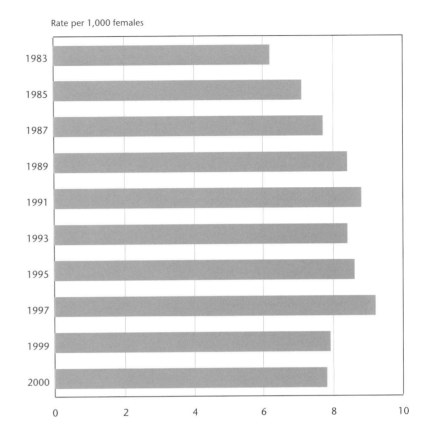

SOURCE: Information and Statistics Division Website. Scottish Health Service, 2001.

4.5 Rates of maternities and abortions in England and Wales among 13-15 year-olds, 1969-2000

Rate per 1,000 females

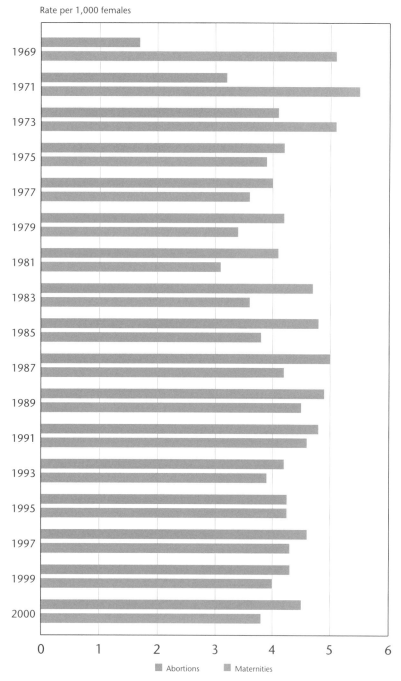

■ Abortions   ■ Maternities

SOURCE: Population Trends. Spring 2002. Office for National Statistics.

Turning now to the older group in England and Wales it can be seen from **Chart 4.6** that again rates of conception have varied over the last decades, but overall there has been a slight decrease during this period. In Scotland rates have stayed relatively stable since 1983, as can be seen from **Chart 4.7**.

In the 15-19 year age group there has been a striking change with regard to the rates of maternities and abortions. As can be seen from **Chart 4.8** maternities have fallen in England and Wales, whilst abortions have increased steadily from the early 1970s. What is not apparent from these figures is the proportion of maternities to abortions in the two age groups. As can be seen from **Chart 4.9** over 50% of conceptions in the younger group lead to abortions, whilst only a third do so in the older group.

Comparable figures are not available for Northern Ireland, but we can see the number of births in this age group since 1985. Rates for women aged 15-19 have varied to some extent, but again within a limited range of between 23 and 30 per thousand women. These figures are shown in **Chart 4.10**.

As has already been noted, Britain compares very poorly with other countries in respect of teenage pregnancy. In July 2001 UNICEF produced a report, as part of their Innocenti Report Card series, entitled "Teenage births in rich countries". This has proved an important and influential publication, illustrating how far the

4.6 Conception rates in England and Wales, 15-19 year-olds, 1969-2000

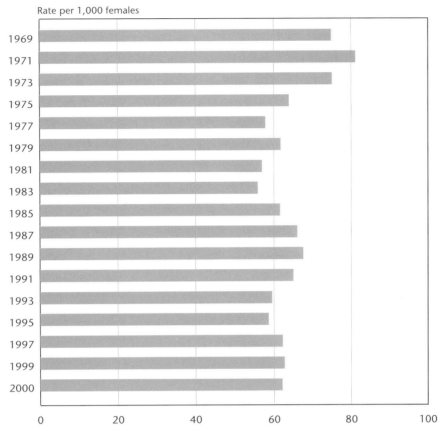

Rate per 1,000 females

SOURCE: Population Trends. Spring 2002. Office for National Statistics.

4.7 Conception rates in Scotland, 16-19 year-olds, 1983-2000

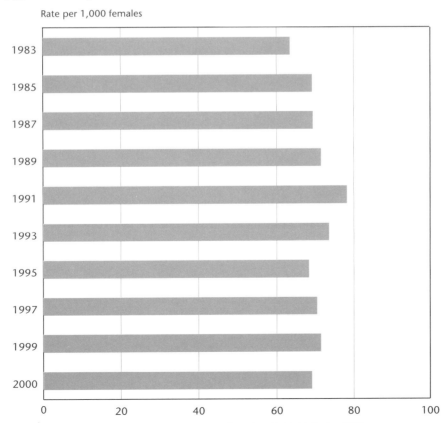

Rate per 1,000 females

SOURCE: Information and Statistics Division Website. Scottish Health Service, 2001.

4.8 Rates of maternities and abortions among women aged 15-19 in England and Wales, 1969-2000

Rate per 1,000 females

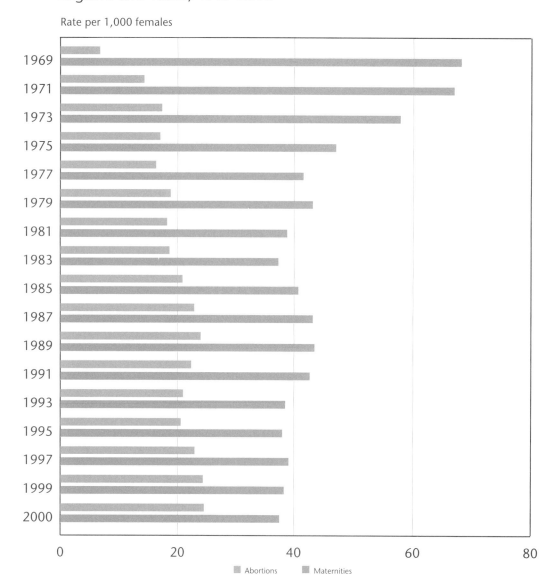

Abortions   Maternities

SOURCE: Population Trends. Spring 2002. Office for National Statistics.

4.9 Proportion of maternities to abortions in England and Wales among two age groups, 2000

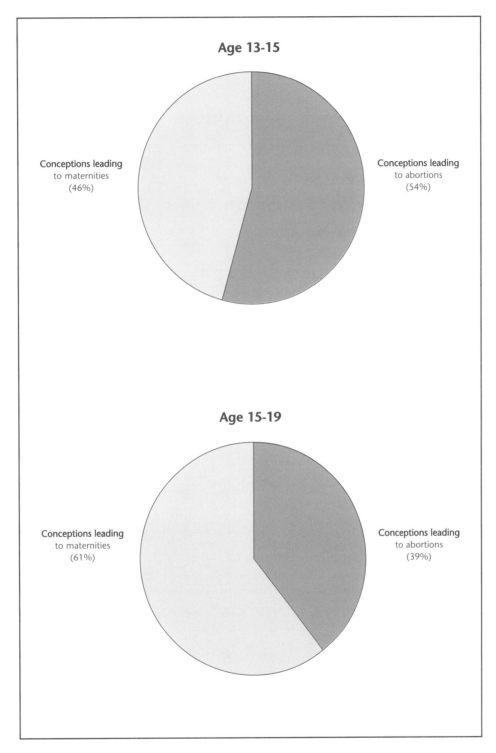

SOURCE: Population Trends. Spring 2002. Office for National Statistics.

4.10 Birth rates for women aged 15-19 in Northern Ireland, 1985-1998

Rate per 1,000 females

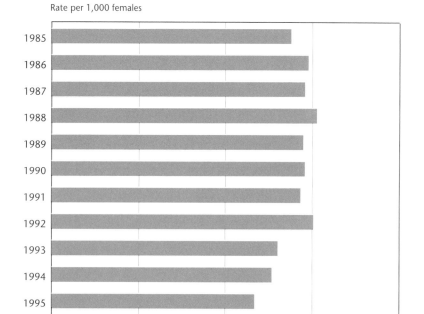

SOURCE: Northern Ireland Registrar's General Annual Report, 1998.

UK has to go to catch up with other countries in this respect. Figures shown in **Chart 4.11** indicate that in 1998, among the 15-17 year age group, Britain had a rate of 16.6 live births per thousand young women. This is a figure which was higher only in the United States. Data shown in **Chart 4.12** illustrate the same phenomenon for those in the 18-19 year age range, indicating a rate of 51.8 births per thousand women in 1998 in the UK. It may be argued that these figures relate only to live births, rather than conceptions. However the UNICEF report gives details of abortions in the different countries as well, showing that not only does Britain have a very high rate of live births among young women, but it also has one of the highest rates of abortions among this group too. Thus, if the two sets of figures are put together, it is apparent that Britain is close to top of the league both in rates of births as well as in rates of conceptions among women under the age of 20.

One important feature of the overall picture is that, as is explained both in the UNICEF report, and in the Social Exclusion report "Teenage Pregnancy" (1999), birth rates in countries such as Germany, France and Italy were very similar to those in the UK in the 1970s. However birth rates among young women aged 15-19 have fallen steadily since that time in most European countries, while rates in Britain have remained at much the same level for the last thirty years. It is not clear why this should be so, but no doubt the standards of sex

4.11 Birth rates for women aged 15-17 in OECD countries, 1998

Rate per 1,000 females

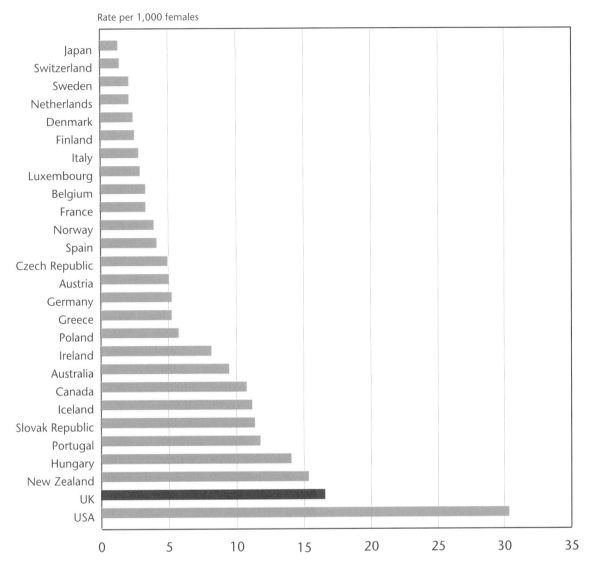

SOURCE: Innocenti Report Card. Issue No. 3. UNICEF, July 2001.

4.12 Birth rates for women aged 18-19 in OECD countries, 1998

Rate per 1,000 females

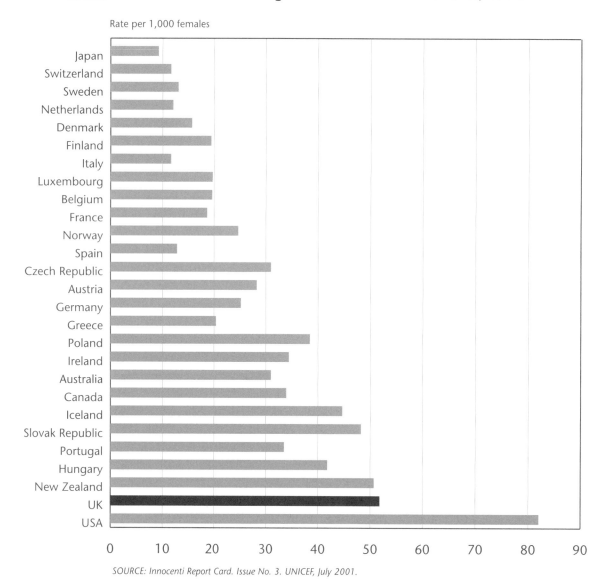

SOURCE: Innocenti Report Card. Issue No. 3. UNICEF, July 2001.

education, the range and accessibility of sexual health services, and attitudes to contraception all play their part in determining rates of live births among young women.

Continuing on the theme of contraception, it can be seen from the data illustrated in **Chart 4.13** that, of those under 16 attending family planning clinics, 37% are on the pill, while 50% are using the condom. In the 16-19 year age group 53% are on the pill. The use of the condom reduces with age, as might be expected. It is interesting to compare these figures with those supplied by Henderson et al. (2002) regarding the sample of 14 year-olds in Scotland. In this study it is reported that 65% of boys and girls said they used a condom at both first and most recent intercourse, with 9% using the withdrawal method, and 3% using emergency contraception. Less than 3% were using the pill. 19% of the sample told the researchers that they had used no contraception at all on first intercourse, and 17% were still using no contraception at the most recent experience of intercourse.

As far as the incidence of sexually transmitted infections is concerned, figures in **Chart 4.14** give a picture of the range of problems which presented at GUM clinics in 2001 across England, Wales and Northern Ireland. As can be seen both chlamydia and genital warts are infections presenting in significant numbers. It is of continuing concern to health professionals that the

4.13 Contraceptive use among women attending family planning clinics, by age, in England, 2001-02

Method				Percentages
	Under 16	16-19	20-24	All ages
Oral contraceptives - total	37	53	55	46
combined preparation	35	50	51	40
progestogen only	2	3	4	6
IUD	0	1	4	7
Cap/diaphragm	0	0	0	1
Injectable contraceptive	4	8	10	9
Other chemicals	0	0	0	0
Male condom	50	31	24	29
Female condom	0	0	0	0
Rhythm method	0	0	0	0
Female sterilisation	0	0	0	0
Implant	0	0	1	1
Other methods	8	7	6	6

SOURCE: Government Statistical Service. Bulletin 2002/20.

4.14 New diagnoses of sexually transmitted infections, by gender and age, in England, 2001

Diagnosis	Under 15		15		16-19	Numbers
	M	F	M	F	M	F
Infectious syphilis (primary and secondary)	0	0	0	1	10	9
Gonorrhoea (uncomplicated)	11	63	40	213	2012	2564
Gonorrhoea (uncomplicated) homosexually acquired	2	-	0	-	144	-
Genital chlamydia (uncomplicated)	25	224	60	729	4177	13,398
Genital herpes (first attack)	2	48	7	99	390	2163
Genital warts (first attack)	42	132	21	344	3350	8805

SOURCE: Trends in Sexually Transmitted Infections in the UK: New Episodes seen at GUM clinics 1996-2001. Public Health Laboratory Service, November 2002.

4.15 New diagnoses of chlamydia infections presented at GUM clinics in England, Wales and Northern Ireland among 16-19 year-olds, by gender, 1996-2001

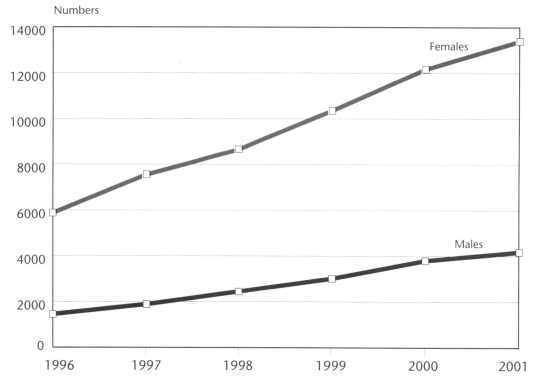

Numbers

SOURCE: Trends in Sexually Transmitted Infections in the UK: New Episodes seen at GUM clinics 1996-2001. Public Health Laboratory Service, November 2002.

4.16 New diagnoses of gonorrhoea infections presented at GUM clinics in England, Wales and Northern Ireland among 16-19 year-olds, by gender, 1996-2001

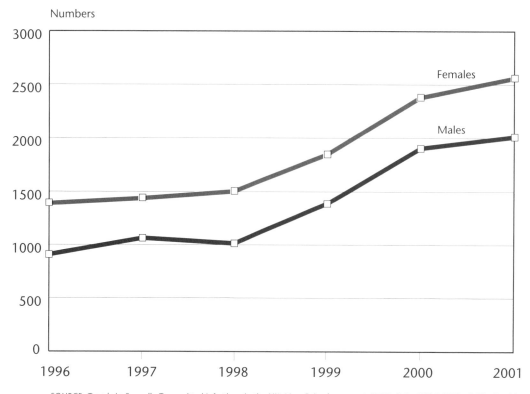

Numbers

SOURCE: Trends in Sexually Transmitted Infections in the UK: New Episodes seen at GUM clinics 1996-2001. Public Health Laboratory Service, November 2002.

incidence of these STIs has shown a dramatic increase over the last few years, especially among older adolescents. Figures in **Charts 4.15** and **4.16** illustrate the trends in rates of chlamydia and gonorrhoea.

Turning now to AIDS and HIV infections, concern has been expressed at the possibility that the rates for these infections are also increasing in this country. The incidence of AIDS itself is low, with a total of 28 males and 46 females under the age of 30 being diagnosed with this condition in 2001 in the UK. This compares with 54 males and 48 females in the same age group being so diagnosed in 1991. However if we look at those diagnosed with HIV infections, we can see that there has been a marked rise over the last decade. Figures shown in **Chart 4.17** indicate that, for those likely to have been infected as a result of heterosexual intercourse, numbers have more than doubled since 1992. Taken together with the increasing rates of other STIs, these figures are a further cause for anxiety.

We will conclude this chapter by looking briefly at knowledge of sexual health services and attitudes to sex education. One striking finding reported in the Exeter survey has to do with teenagers' awareness of birth control services. Figures in **Chart 4.18** indicate the low numbers of adolescents who are aware of such services. Among 14 and 15 year-olds 61% of boys and 45% of girls do not know whether such services are available in their locality. This is a very worrying statistic, and among

4.17 Numbers of HIV infected individuals: infections probably acquired through sexual intercourse between men and women, by age and gender, 1992-2001

Numbers

Males				
Age group	1992	1995	1998	2001
15 - 19	1	5	3	14
20 - 24	28	24	20	40
25 - 29	84	75	60	150

Females				
Age group	1992	1995	1998	2001
15 - 19	10	8	18	46
20 - 24	122	61	70	211
25 - 29	134	151	183	420

SOURCE: AIDS/HIV Quarterly Surveillance Tables. Cumulative UK Data to End September 2002. Public Health Laboratory Service AIDS Centre and the Scottish Centre for Infection & Environmental Health.

4.18 Answers to the question, "Is there a special birth control service for young people available locally?", among Year 10 pupils

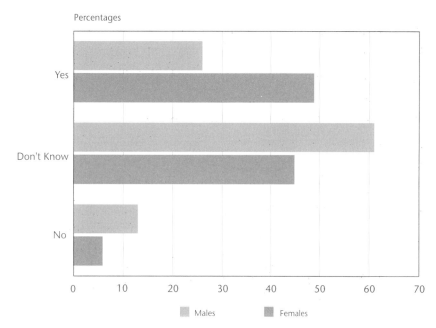

Percentages

SOURCE: Balding (2002).

other things reflects on the topics taught in school in relation to sexual health. If we really wish to reduce rates of teenage pregnancy then there is little doubt that improving knowledge of sexual health services among young people is one objective that needs some attention.

Let us look now at attitudes to sex education. Information presented in **Chart 4.19** indicates that teenagers, by the time they reach the age of 15, are gaining most of their knowledge from school and the peer group. About 20% indicate that magazines and other media are the main source of information. As for parents, more girls than boys cite their families, but even among girls only 34% of 12 and 13 year-olds and 20% of 14 and 15 year-olds see their parents as providing information about sex. This contrasts starkly with evidence about what young people want. The Exeter study shows that between 40% and 50% of girls want their parents to be the main source of information about sex, while almost as many boys feel the same way. It is clear that parents could play a greater role here, if only there was appropriate support to assist them in this task.

4.19 Proportions indicating their main and preferred source of information about sex, by age and gender, in England, 2001

Percentages

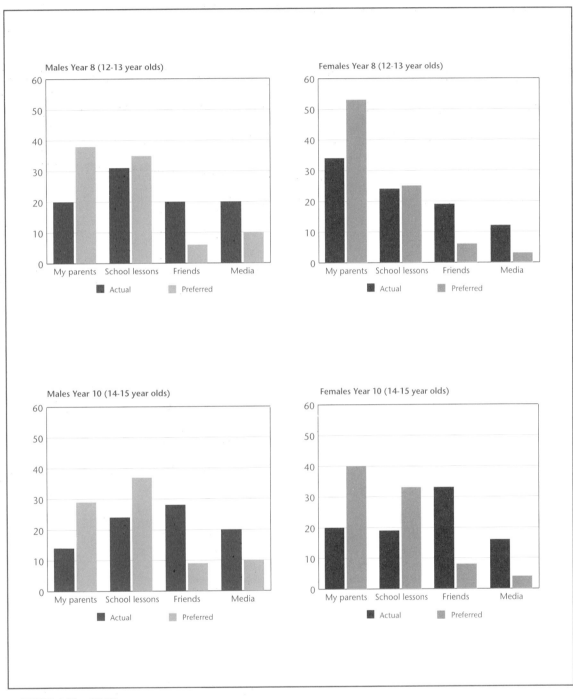

SOURCE: Balding (2002).

References

Balding, J (2002) Young people in 2001. Exeter Health Education Unit. University of Exeter.

Farrell, C (1978) My mother said .... Routledge. London.

Henderson, M et al. (2002) Heterosexual risk behaviour among young people in Scotland. Journal of Adolescence. 25. 483-494.

Johnson, A et al. (1994) Sexual attitudes and lifestyles. Blackwells. Oxford.

Schofield, M (1965) The sexual behaviour of young people. Longmans. London.

Wellings, K et al. (2001) Sexual behaviour in Britain: early heterosexual experience. The Lancet. 358. 1843-1850.

Wight, D and Henderson, M (2000) Extent of regretted sexual intercourse among young teenagers in Scotland. British Medical Journal. 320. 1243-1244.

_____(1999) Teenage pregnancy: a report by the Social Exclusion Unit. The Stationery Office. London.

Chapter 5

Mental Health

Mental Health

Issues to do with the mental health of children and young people have been receiving considerably more attention in the past few years than was the case during the 1990s. This is partly as a result of the establishment of the Children's Taskforce, and the drive to establish a Children's National Service Framework (NSF). One of the six external working groups assisting in drawing up the Children's NSF is concerned with mental health and psychological well-being. During the summer of 2002 the Chancellor announced considerable extra funding for the National Health Service, and it is understood that at least some of this will go to child and adolescent mental health services. In addition the Government has established the National Institute of Mental Health, and this body, in conjunction with a range of initiatives originating from within the Royal College of Psychiatrists, will have the effect of raising the profile of mental health issues. Finally a range of voluntary organizations, especially Young Minds and the Mental Health Foundation, have been active in pressing for more effective services and in identifying particular areas of need.

In this chapter we will start with a look at the statistics on suicide. It has been the hope and intention of all Governments throughout the last decade to be able to reduce the suicide rates, especially the rates among young men. Looking at the rates for the UK as a whole, as shown in **Chart 5.1**, it can be seen that there has been no dramatic decrease in recent years, although there has been a small decline in rates for young men between 1997 and 2000. Rates for young men in England and Wales have, however, shown a more marked decrease between 1997 and 2000, down from 16 per 100,000 to 12 per 100,000, as can be seen in **Chart 5.2**. This will provide some encouragement to those who have been given the task of implementing the current National Suicide Prevention Strategy.

On a less optimistic note, it can be seen from figures in **Chart 5.3** that in some regions of the UK rates are increasing rather than decreasing. Thus in Scotland rates for young men have risen from 23 per 100,000 in 1990 to 36 per 100,000 in 2000. Figures in **Chart 5.4** show a similar worrying trend in Northern Ireland, and much the same is true of the Republic of Ireland, as is illustrated in **Chart 5.5**. If we wish to understand suicidal behaviour it is clearly essential to consider regional trends, and any effective suicide prevention strategy will need to take into account factors relevant to the conditions of life in the different countries of the UK.

It may be suggested that a discussion of rates is not a sufficiently powerful reflection of the real nature of the problem. While we can say that rates look as if they are falling in England and Wales, behind these statistics lie a catalogue of human misery and despair. A more graphic expression of the problem is to consider the actual figures, and to recognize that in 2000 a total of 555 young men in the UK between the ages of 15 and 24 took their lives as

5.1 Suicide rates in the UK among 15-24 year-olds, 1990-2000

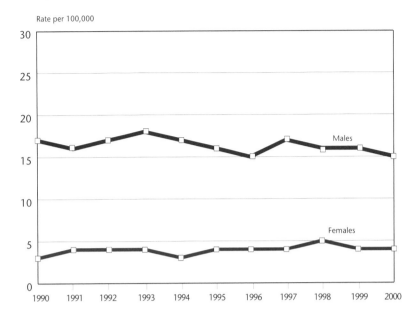

SOURCE: Office for National Statistics, General Register Office for Scotland, General Register Office for Northern Ireland, Central Statistics Office Ireland.

5.2 Suicide rates in England and Wales among 15-24 year-olds, 1990-2000

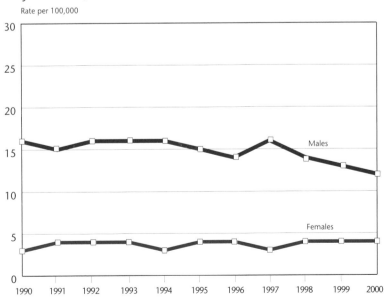

SOURCE: Office for National Statistics.

5.3 Suicide rates in Scotland among 15-24 year-olds, 1990-2000

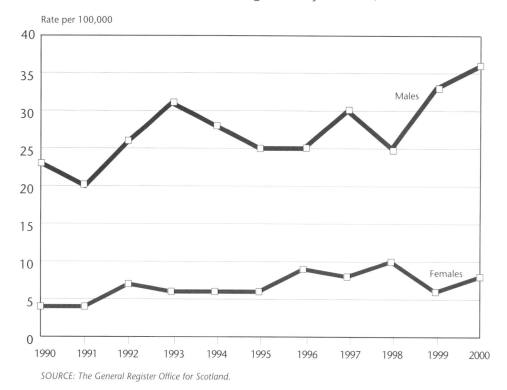

Rate per 100,000

SOURCE: The General Register Office for Scotland.

5.4 Suicide rates in Northern Ireland among 15-24 year-olds, 1990-2000

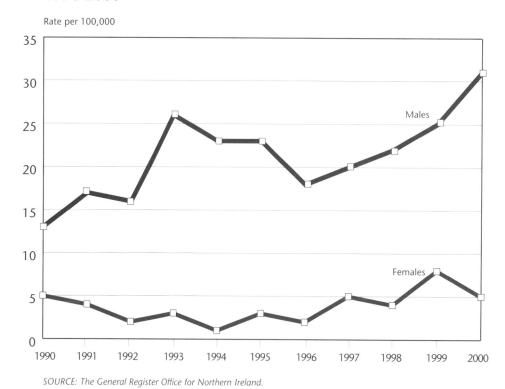

Rate per 100,000

SOURCE: The General Register Office for Northern Ireland.

5.5 Suicide rates in the Republic of Ireland among 15-24 year-olds, 1990-2000

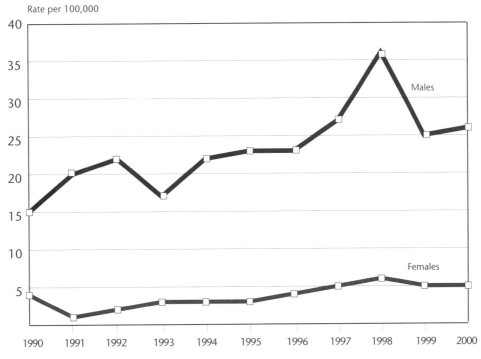

Rate per 100,000

SOURCE: Central Statistics Office, Ireland.

5.6 Number of suicides and undetermined deaths in the UK, by age and gender

Numbers

	1991	1995	2000
Male			
0-14	18	17	21
15-24	731	601	555
25-34	1031	1154	1037
Female			
0-14	4	15	11
15-24	142	139	143
25-34	263	242	258

SOURCE: Office for National Statistics, General Register Office for Scotland, General Register Office for Northern Ireland, Central Statistics Office Ireland.

5.7 Suicide rates among 15-24 year-olds in different countries, 1995-2000 (latest available year)

Rate per 100,000

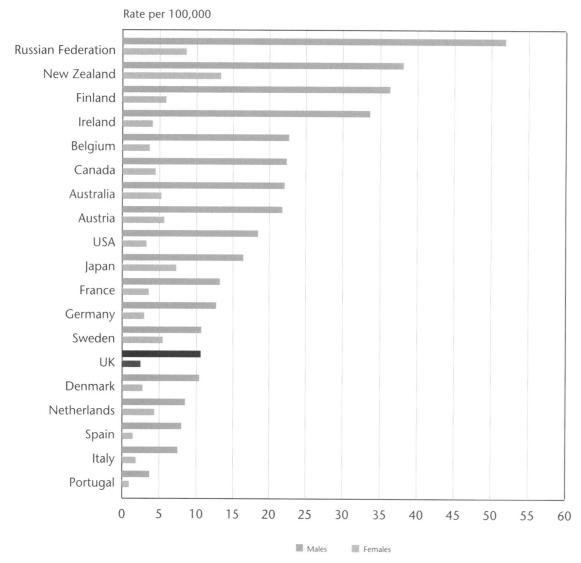

SOURCE: Figures and facts about suicide. World Health Organisation. Geneva. 2002.

a result of suicide. Comparisons of the actual figures for completed suicides in the UK between 1991, 1995 and 2000 are shown in **Chart 5.6.**

Turning now to international comparisons, figures in **Chart 5.7** show that, while rates in the UK are higher than in some other European countries, there are others that have rates substantially higher than in Britain, such as Finland, and New Zealand. However it is a sobering thought that Finland, with an annual rate of 36 per 100,000 young men committing suicide annually, has the same rate as Scotland.

It will be obvious that information on the rate of attempted suicide is more difficult to obtain than rates for completed suicides. Professor Keith Hawton and colleagues recently carried out a large study of nearly 6,000 young people for the Samaritans, asking about the prevalence of deliberate self-harm and suicidal ideation in the previous year. Some findings from this study are illustrated in **Chart 5.8**, showing that 3.2% of young men and 11.2% of young women report an episode of self-harm within a twelve-month period.

This evidence supports the views of Kerfoot (1996) and McClure (2001) that attempted suicide is much more common in females than in males. The most frequent method used is self-poisoning, usually through an overdose of tablets. While self-report data are useful, it is still difficult to be sure of the actual numbers involved in this type of behaviour. Hawton has estimated that there may be as many as 20,000 young people a year in England and Wales who end up in

5.8 Prevalence of deliberate self-harm and suicidal ideation in previous year, based on descriptions provided by adolescents

	No. of respondents	No.	(%)
Deliberate self-harm:			
Males	3078	98	(3.2)
Females	2703	299	(11.2)
All*	5801	398	(6.9)
Suicidal ideation (no self-harm):			
Males	3025	258	(8.5)
Females	2692	602	(22.4)
All*	5737	863	(15.0)
No self-harm or suicidal thoughts:			
Males	3025	2669	(88.2)
Females	2692	1791	(66.5)
All*	5737	4476	(78.0)

* Twenty people did not indicate gender

SOURCE: Hawton et al. (2002).

5.9 Number of individuals under the age of 19 referred to general hospital in Oxford as a result of deliberate self-harm, 1985-1995

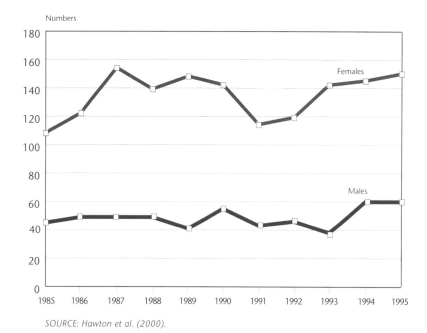

Numbers

SOURCE: Hawton et al. (2000).

Accident and Emergency hospital departments as a result of an episode of attempted suicide. Recently he and colleagues published a study (Hawton et al., 2000) which reported on findings from the Oxford region. The study looked at the numbers of young men and young women being referred to hospital because of attempted suicide, and some of the findings are illustrated in **Chart 5.9**. Results show that numbers varied over a decade, with some moderate increase between 1985 and 1995, but that females outnumbered males consistently.

Turning now to the prevalence of psychiatric disorder, it is useful that in the last few years more evidence on this question has become available. First Meltzer et al. (2000) studied children and young people up to the age of 15, and then Singleton et al. (2001) have reported on a study of adults in England, Wales and Scotland, with the sample commencing at age 16. Looking first at the Meltzer study, this also covered England, Wales and Scotland, and involved more than 10,000 children and young people. Figures in **Chart 5.10** illustrate the overall prevalence rates for different types of disorder among 11-15 year-olds. As will be apparent, rates of emotional disorder are higher in girls, while rates of conduct disorder are substantially higher in boys.

The study provides a wealth of data on various aspects of psychiatric disorder, and two details of the findings are illustrated in **Charts 5.11** and **5.12**. In the first of these, disorders are distributed according to ethnic group, and from this it can be seen that rates of disorder are

5.10 Prevalence of mental disorders in 11-15 year-olds in the UK, by gender, 1999

Percentages

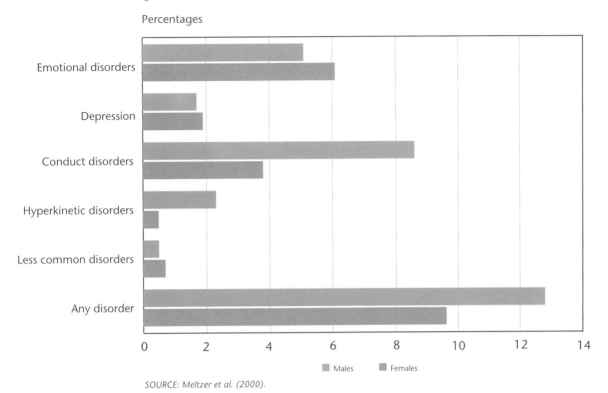

SOURCE: Meltzer et al. (2000).

5.11 Prevalence of mental disorder among 11-15 year-olds, by ethnicity

Percentages

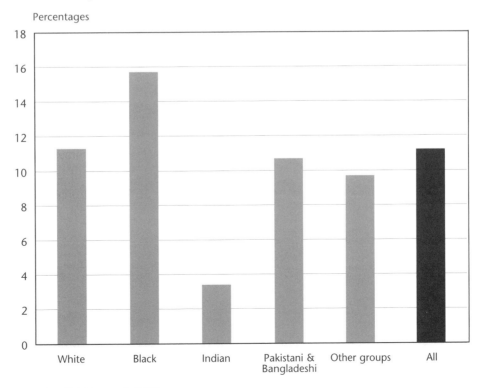

SOURCE: Meltzer et al. (2000).

5.12 Prevalence of mental disorder among 11-15 year-olds, by social class of family

Percentages

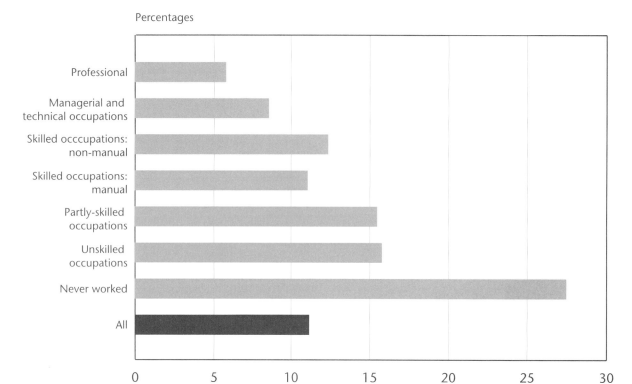

SOURCE: Meltzer et al. (2000).

higher among Black young people, and are very much lower among Indian adolescents. In the second chart disorders are distributed across social class categories. These findings are particularly striking, illustrating how closely disorder is linked to social class in Britain.

As far as rates of disorder among older age groups are concerned, the recent study by Singleton et al. (2001) provides a range of valuable information, although it is unfortunate that the sample is so small for the 16-19 year age group. We look first at the prevalence of probable psychotic disorder, illustrated in **Chart 5.13**. Here it can be seen that there is very little change across the age span for females, but that rates for men show a substantial increase once they reach their thirties. Another way of looking at this is to state that rates among 16-19 year-olds and 20-24 year-olds reflect morbidity among women but not among men in these age bands.

We now turn to the prevalence of neurotic disorders, illustrated across the age range in **Chart 5.14**. Generalized anxiety disorder increases with age for both men and women, as do depressive episodes in men. Women show little change across the age span for depressive episodes, nor for any of the other neurotic conditions. It is of note that most neurotic conditions are more prevalent in women than in men. The last piece of evidence drawn from this study and illustrated in **Chart 5.15** is the picture gained by looking at those having a score of more than two on 14 neurotic symptoms derived from the use of the revised version of the Clinical

5.13 Prevalence of probable psychotic disorder, by age and gender

Rates per 1,000 in past year

	Females	Males
16-19	5	-
20-24	4	-
25-29	2	-
30-34	4	13
35-39	8	8
40-44	12	7
45-49	6	5
50-54	5	9
55-59	-	10
60-64	1	7
65-69	6	-
70-74	2	4
All	5	6

SOURCE: Singleton, N et al. (2001).

5.14 Prevalence of neurotic disorders, by age and gender

Rates per 1,000 in past week*

	16-19	20-24	25-29	30-34	35-39	40-44	45-49	50-54	55-59	60-64	65-69	70-74	All
Females													
Mixed anxiety and depressive disorder	124	138	131	115	92	127	98	126	75	87	83	68	108
Generalised anxiety disorder	11	18	48	39	54	64	54	73	58	45	37	30	46
Depressive episode	27	35	21	30	39	26	28	33	46	14	10	17	28
All phobias	21	15	26	22	35	30	22	27	14	16	13	4	22
Obsessive compulsive disorder	9	18	16	13	18	18	15	7	17	15	5	4	13
Panic disorder	6	-	12	6	6	5	9	15	10	-	7	7	7
Any neurotic disorder	**192**	**209**	**216**	**205**	**191**	**229**	**188**	**246**	**176**	**148**	**147**	**119**	**194**
Base	*151*	*258*	*398*	*574*	*564*	*460*	*363*	*435*	*389*	*407*	*373*	*356*	*4728*
Males													
Mixed anxiety and depressive disorder	51	44	93	59	85	89	85	62	61	72	35	41	68
Generalised anxiety disorder	16	11	32	52	53	58	87	59	40	39	14	16	43
Depressive episode	9	8	27	12	36	30	44	32	22	35	2	5	23
All phobias	6	19	11	18	17	12	28	13	12	12	-	4	13
Obsessive compulsive disorder	9	20	8	8	8	9	10	7	11	12	-	-	9
Panic disorder	5	8	8	8	5	5	11	8	18	4	-	-	7
Any neurotic disorder	**86**	**100**	**152**	**130**	**154**	**162**	**204**	**150**	**134**	**145**	**50**	**66**	**135**
Base	*183*	*202*	*332*	*379*	*442*	*382*	*360*	*387*	*314*	*332*	*295*	*244*	*3852*

* People may have more than one type of disorder.

SOURCE: Singleton, N et al. (2001).

5.15 Proportion of those having a score of two or more on symptoms derived from the Clinical Interview Schedule (CIS-R), by age and gender

Percentages

	16-19	20-24	25-29	30-34	35-39	40-44	45-49	50-54	55-59	60-64	65-69	70-74	All
Females													
Sleep problems	36	32	31	30	32	34	36	37	38	35	37	36	34
Fatigue	35	31	33	33	32	37	29	42	30	26	25	26	32
Irritability	35	29	28	28	26	24	19	20	17	12	10	6	22
Worry	28	26	24	21	22	26	22	23	19	18	12	10	21
Depression	16	11	11	14	13	14	9	12	11	7	10	7	12
Concentration and forgetfullness	13	11	9	13	11	12	11	15	9	7	6	6	11
Depressive ideas	20	12	12	12	13	14	9	12	10	7	4	4	11
Anxiety	7	8	10	9	9	11	10	13	11	8	7	6	9
Somatic symptoms	4	9	10	9	10	9	9	10	9	6	5	5	8
Worry - Physical health	8	10	6	7	7	8	5	9	8	7	6	8	7
Obsessions	7	7	10	9	9	9	6	5	4	6	4	6	7
Phobias	8	6	7	7	6	8	3	8	5	4	4	3	6
Compulsions	5	4	5	3	4	5	2	3	3	3	2	3	4
Panic	2	1	2	2	2	4	2	3	2	2	1	1	2
Base	*151*	*258*	*398*	*574*	*564*	*460*	*363*	*435*	*389*	*407*	*373*	*356*	*4728*
Males													
Sleep problems	23	23	28	22	25	25	27	22	25	23	18	19	24
Fatigue	15	16	27	22	26	24	29	21	23	25	17	17	23
Irritability	15	17	23	19	24	20	23	19	15	14	7	5	18
Worry	11	13	20	21	19	17	21	21	14	13	8	7	17
Depression	8	8	11	7	12	13	15	10	10	13	6	4	10
Concentration and forgetfullness	4	6	9	10	10	10	11	12	9	11	6	6	9
Depressive ideas	7	7	10	8	10	9	10	8	7	8	2	4	8
Anxiety	6	4	8	9	8	10	12	11	6	7	2	3	8
Somatic symptoms	3	1	5	5	6	9	11	7	4	6	3	2	5
Worry - Physical health	4	2	5	6	6	8	10	8	9	10	5	6	7
Obsessions	5	6	5	3	4	3	5	4	4	5	2	2	4
Phobias	5	6	4	4	5	2	4	4	2	2	1	1	3
Compulsions	3	3	2	4	2	2	2	2	2	3	1	1	2
Panic	3	1	2	2	2	2	4	1	2	1	0	0	2
Base	*183*	*202*	*332*	*379*	*442*	*382*	*360*	*387*	*314*	*332*	*295*	*244*	*3852*

SOURCE: Singleton, N et al. (2001).

5.16 Experiences of being bullied for young people aged 11-15, by gender, 1997

Percentages

	Males	Females
Never been bullied	51	47
Been bullied in the past but not this term	23	31
Been bullied this term:		
once or twice	13	13
sometimes	4	4
about once a week	2	2
several times a week	3	2
Not stated	4	1
Base (=100%)	*5063*	*5241*

SOURCE: Haselden, Angle and Hickman (1999).

5.17 Numbers on Child Protection Registers by age, in England, 1991-2001

Numbers

		Age at 31 March				
	All ages	Under 1	1 - 4	5 - 9	10 - 15	16 & over
1991	45,300	2,800	14,600	14,500	11,700	1,700
1992	38,600	2,500	12,000	12,200	10,400	1,500
1993	32,500	2,300	9,900	10,000	9,100	1,100
1994	34,900	2,700	10,500	10,700	9,700	1,000
1995	35,000	2,900	10,800	10,600	9,600	900
1996	32,400	2,600	9,900	10,000	8,800	900
1997	32,400	2,800	9,800	10,000	8,700	800
1998	31,600	2,800	9,600	9,800	8,500	700
1999	31,900	3,000	9,700	9,700	8,600	600
2000	30,300	2,800	9,200	9,100	8,400	600
2001	28,600	2,800	8,000	8,000	7,400	600

SOURCE: Children and Young People on Child Protection Registers – year ending 31 March 2001. A/F 00/13. Department of Health.

Interview Schedule (CIS-R). Results show that there are more women having high scores on depression, depressive ideas and irritability in the 16-19 year age group than in any other age group.

Bullying in school is an important issue with implications for the mental health of young people. For obvious reasons statistics are hard to collect, but a number of surveys do include questions about this topic. One of the most extensive surveys is the one carried out by Haselden et al. (1999), and information about bullying from this study is set out in **Chart 5.16**. From this it can be seen that in the region of 20% of secondary school pupils report being bullied at some time during a school term. However only a small proportion of this group are bullied once or more than once a week. In this survey there appears to be little gender difference in the experience of being bullied.

Turning now to the even more serious problem of abuse, estimates vary widely as to the extent of this, and it is difficult to obtain any figures which can be considered completely reliable. What is available is the number of those on child protection registers, and these are set out in **Chart 5.17**. From this it can be seen that there is an approximately equal distribution between the ages of 1-4, 5-9 and 10-15. Those who are over 16 form a small proportion of the total.

To end this chapter we will look at the results of a question posed in the Exeter survey (Balding, 2002) on young people's worries. From the results illustrated in **Chart 5.18** it can be seen that girls worry more than boys, and that the extent of worries increases with age. Many adolescents worry about family and friends, and in addition the older group of teenagers worry about school work and the way they look. It is a striking fact that over 50% of girls aged 14-15 worry about their appearance, and that one in three young people are worrying about school work and career problems at this age.

5.18 Proportions of 10-15 year-olds responding "A lot/Quite a lot" to the question: "How much do you worry about these problems?"

Percentages

	Males			Females		
	10-11	12-13	14-15	10-11	12-13	14-15
School problems	16	22	29	16	22	39
Health problems	20	20	17	23	27	28
Career problems	*	20	28	*	18	36
Problems with friends	*	17	15	*	33	33
Family problems	23	22	24	28	33	41
The way you look	15	23	24	28	45	55
HIV/AIDS	*	11	13	*	13	16
Puberty and growing up	13	15	11	27	25	16
The environment	20	*	*	20	*	*
None of these	47	45	39	39	28	19

* Options not available

SOURCE: Balding (2002).

References

Balding, J (2002) Young people in 2001. Schools Health Education Unit. Exeter.

Haselden, L, Angle, H and Hickman, M (1999) Young people and health: health behaviour in school-aged children. Health Education Authority. London.

Hawton, K et al. (2000) Deliberate self-harm in adolescents in Oxford 1985-1995. Journal of Adolescence. 23. 47-55.

Hawton, K et al. (2002) Deliberate self-harm in adolescents: self report survey in schools in England. British Medical Journal. 325. 1207-1211.

Kerfoot, M (1996) Suicide and deliberate self-harm in children and adolescents. Children and Society. 10. 236-241.

McClure, G (2001) Suicide in children and adolescents in England and Wales 1970-1998. British Journal of Psychiatry. 178. 469-474.

Meltzer, H et al. (2000) Mental health of children and adolescents in Great Britain. Office for National Statistics. Stationery Office. London.

Singleton, N et al. (2001) Psychiatric morbidity among adults living in private households, 2000. The Stationery Office. London.

Chapter 6

Crime

Crime

Youth crime arouses as much public concern as almost any other aspect of adolescent behaviour. Fears that growing numbers of young people are becoming involved in offending have been widespread for many years, and as a result new policies are continually being introduced into the youth justice field. There has been much debate about the efficacy of custody in contrast to community sentences, and increasingly governments have sought ways to ensure that parents take greater responsibility for the criminal behaviour of their sons and daughters.

In the recent past, since the Labour government was elected in 1997, we have seen a more radical reform of the youth justice system than any that has been introduced over the last fifty years. Many of these reforms were set out in the legislation incorporated in the Crime and Disorder Act 1998. This established the Youth Justice Board, and introduced a range of new sentences, including the Detention and Training Order, the Final Warning, the Reparation Order and the Parenting Order. The Board has been charged with finding ways of reducing offending, of streamlining court procedures, of monitoring the work of the new multi-disciplinary teams (youth offending teams), and improving the standard of secure provision for juveniles given a custodial sentence.

Clearly there is enormous interest in whether these reforms are having the desired effect. Particular focus is

6.1 Persons found guilty of, or cautioned for, indictable offences per 100,000 population, by age and gender, in England and Wales, 2001

Numbers per 100,000

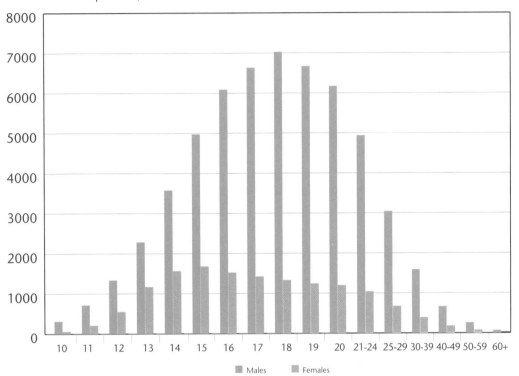

SOURCE: Criminal Statistics, England and Wales, 2001. Research, Development & Statistics Directorate and National Statistics. © Crown Copyright 2002.

6.2 Persons found guilty of, or cautioned for, indictable offences per 100,000 population, by age group, in England and Wales, 1991-2001

Males

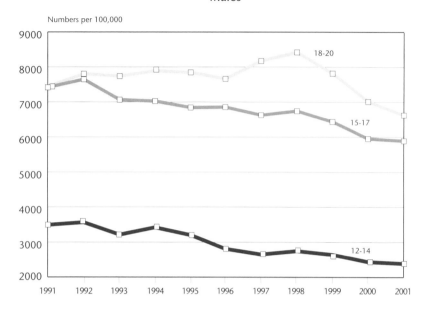

Numbers per 100,000

Females

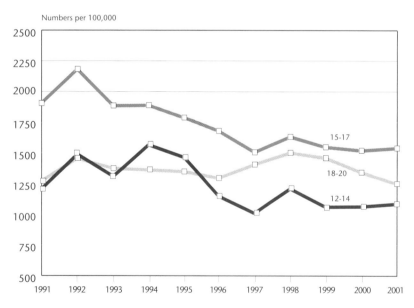

Numbers per 100,000

SOURCE: Criminal Statistics, England and Wales, 2001. Research, Development & Statistics Directorate and National Statistics. © Crown Copyright 2002.

directed towards questions such as whether there has been any decrease in repeat offending, whether court procedures have been streamlined, whether the time between arrest and sentence has been reduced, and whether secure conditions for juveniles are improving. In spite of high hopes that evidence will quickly be found of the beneficial impact of the reforms, it is obvious that some time will be needed before such substantial changes in the youth justice system lead to root and branch improvement. Furthermore many of the new sentences, such as Final Warnings, Detention and Training Orders, and Reparation Orders have only been available to the courts since 2000 or 2001.

Nonetheless, as will be apparent from the data illustrated in this chapter, there is some encouraging evidence showing a reduction in youth crime over the period 1991 to 2001. Almost all age groups under the age of 21 show a gradual decline in the numbers of those found guilty or cautioned for indictable offences. There is, as yet, not enough evidence to link such change directly to the reforms of the youth justice system, but the trend is certainly in the right direction.

In looking at the data the first figures to be considered here have to do with the peak age of offending. As will be clear from **Chart 6.1** there is a significant difference between males and females in rates of offending. For young men offending reaches a peak at age 18, while for young women much the same level of offending can be seen between the ages of 14 and 19, with a peak at age 15.

6.3 Offenders cautioned for indictable offences as a percentage of offenders found guilty or cautioned, by year and age group, in England and Wales

Percentages

Year	Males					Females				
	10-11	12-14	15-17	18-20	21 & over	10-11	12-14	15-17	18-20	21 & over
1991	96	85	55	23	18	99	94	76	41	40
1992	96	86	59	29	23	99	96	81	50	46
1993	96	83	59	32	26	99	95	80	52	46
1994	95	81	56	34	25	100	94	77	50	44
1995	94	79	54	35	26	99	93	76	51	44
1996	94	77	51	35	26	99	91	72	50	44
1997	93	74	49	35	26	98	89	68	48	42
1998	91	72	48	34	24	97	88	67	46	39
1999	87	69	45	31	22	96	87	64	43	36
2000	86	68	43	29	20	95	86	63	41	34
2001	86	66	42	28	19	95	85	64	41	32

SOURCE: Criminal Statistics, England and Wales, 2001. Research, Development & Statistics Directorate and National Statistics.
© Crown Copyright 2002.

6.4 Offenders found guilty or cautioned, by type of offence, gender and age group, in England and Wales, 2001

Thousands

	Males				Females			
	12-14	15-17	18-20	21 & over	12-14	15-17	18-20	21 & over
Indictable offences								
Violence against the person	3.3	8.8	7.9	26.6	1.2	1.8	0.9	3.9
Sexual offences	0.4	0.6	0.4	3.6	0.0	0.0	0.0	0.1
Burglary	3.6	6.3	5.1	13.6	0.4	0.5	0.3	0.6
Robbery	0.8	2.0	1.4	2.4	0.1	0.3	0.1	0.2
Theft and handling stolen goods	12.6	22.6	20.8	79.8	8.2	9.6	6.9	27.3
Fraud and forgery	0.2	1.3	2.7	12.5	0.2	0.6	1.0	5.6
Criminal damage	1.7	2.4	1.9	6.0	0.3	0.3	0.1	0.8
Drug offences	1.5	10.2	17.4	47.0	0.2	0.9	1.6	6.2
Other (excluding motoring offences)	0.9	4.0	7.9	28.2	0.2	0.6	0.9	4.4
Motoring offences	0.1	0.6	1.2	5.4	-	0.0	0.0	0.4
Total	25	58.9	66.6	225.1	0.8	14.5	11.9	49.4

SOURCE: Criminal Statistics, England and Wales, 2001. Research, Development & Statistics Directorate and National Statistics. © Crown Copyright 2002.

As far as the numbers of young people found guilty or cautioned for indictable offences in the period 1991-2001 are concerned, it can be seen from the figures in **Chart 6.2** that there has been a small but definite decline in such numbers over the past decade. Taking the 15-17 year age group as an example, the rates for young men cautioned or found guilty have declined from 7,416 per 100,000 in 1991 to 5,891 per 100,000 in 2001. For young women the rates have diminished from 1,905 per 100,000 to 1,541 per 100,000. Similar trends can be seen in other age groups, especially among males in the 12-14 year age group.

Turning now to those cautioned as a percentage of those found guilty, it will be seen from figures in **Chart 6.3** that there has been some decrease in the use of this disposal by the courts for males, particularly for those in the younger groups. A similar but rather less marked trend can be seen for females in the 12-14 and 15-17 year age groups. However with the introduction of the Final Warning scheme these figures may begin to look very different in another few years.

A consideration of the data illustrated in **Chart 6.4** indicates how high a percentage of all offences among this age group involves theft and burglary. In the youngest groups these offences account for over 50% of all offences, but this does reduce with age. It is also notable that drug offences as a proportion of all offences increase with age, especially in men. Drug offences in males between 18 and 20 account for nearly 25% of all offences in this age group. Of course

6.5 Changing pattern of sentencing for persons aged 15-17 sentenced for indictable offences, by gender, in England and Wales, 1991-2001

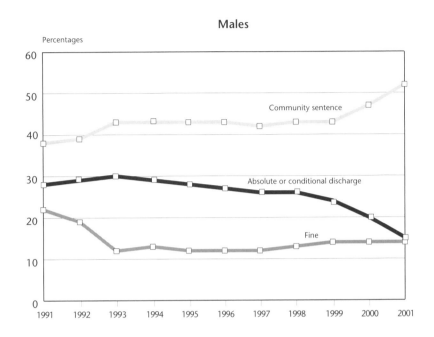

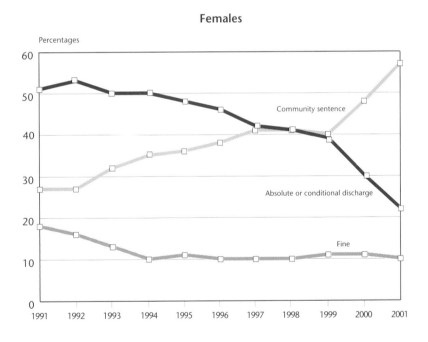

SOURCE: Criminal Statistics, England and Wales, 2001. Research, Development & Statistics Directorate and National Statistics. © Crown Copyright 2002.

6.6 Persons aged 15-17 sentenced for indictable offences, by type of order and gender, in England and Wales, in 2000 and 2001

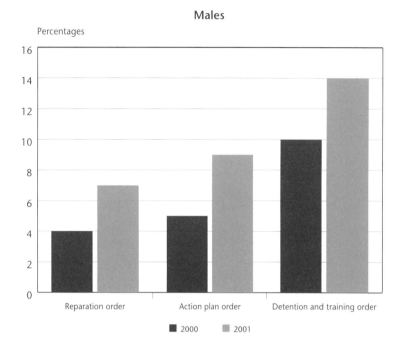

Males

Percentages

2000 2001

Females

Percentages

2000 2001

SOURCE: Criminal Statistics, England and Wales, 2001. Research, Development & Statistics Directorate and National Statistics. © Crown Copyright 2002.

these figures may alter substantially if Parliament agrees later this year to the reclassification of cannabis as a Class C drug, as discussed in Chapter 3.

We now turn to a consideration of sentencing, perhaps one of the most striking illustrations of the impact of the recent youth justice reforms. Firstly we show the change over the last decade in the use of absolute and conditional discharges, fines, and community sentences. As will be apparent from **Chart 6.5** the use by the courts of fines and discharges has declined, whilst the use of community sentences has been on an upward trend over the decade.

As has been noted earlier in the chapter, the use of the new sentencing options, such as the Detention and Training Order, the Reparation Order, and the Action Plan Order, have only been in use for the last year or two, Nonetheless the changes are dramatic. As is shown in **Chart 6.6** these new options are being used already, and will no doubt come to play a larger and larger part in the sentencing policies of courts across the country.

Turning now to custodial sentences, there has been general concern over the increase in the prison population in the UK over the last five years, and this concern is felt particularly strongly where young offenders are concerned. As far as the proportions being given a custodial sentence, it can be seen from the figures in **Chart 6.7** that these have risen slowly but surely for both males and females between 1992 and 2001. We can also consider the numbers held in custody between 1991 and 2002, as shown in **Chart 6.8.** For males there has been an increase from 5,683 to 8,608 and for females from 110 to 464 in a decade. This increase is of serious concern, particularly if it is understood that approximately 25% of these are under the age of 18. In 2002 there are estimated to have been 2,609 juveniles (between the ages of 15 and 17) in prison service establishments in England and Wales, a figure that has doubled since 1992.

There has been concern that the introduction of the Detention and Training Order would have the effect of increasing the numbers in custody, since magistrates may see the option as a beneficial one because of the community element within the sentence. The rising numbers in prison establishments over the last two years give some encouragement to these fears, although as we have noted the Detention and Training Order was only introduced in 2001. Thus the evidence is still to come regarding the long-term effect of the Order.

Anyone concerned about the effects of custody has pointed to the high reconviction rates for young offenders as a clear counter-indication against this type of sentence. Most recent figures are illustrated in **Chart 6.9**, showing that 76% of young men who have had a custodial sentence in 1997 re-offend within two years, while a somewhat lower figure of 58% of females do so.

Recent reports, such as that published by the Social Exclusion Unit in 2002 entitled "Reducing re-offending by ex-prisoners", have focused on the characteristics of those in young offender institutions.

6.7 Custodial sentences for those aged 15-20 in England and Wales, by gender, as a percentage of all those sentenced or cautioned by the courts, 1992-2001

Aged 15-17 years

Percentages

Aged 18-20 years

Percentages

SOURCE: Criminal Statistics, England and Wales, 2001. Research, Development & Statistics Directorate and National Statistics. © Crown Copyright 2002.

6.8 Numbers of young offenders under sentence in Young Offender Institutions, by gender, 1991, 1995, 2000 and 2002

Numbers

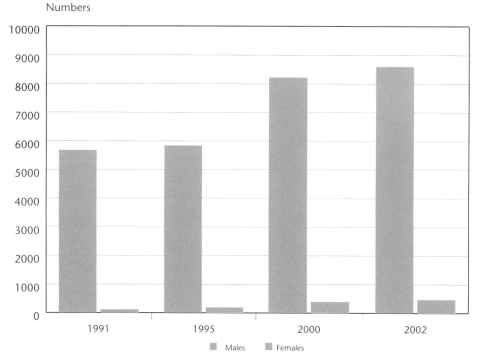

Males ■ Females

SOURCE: Criminal Statistics, 1995; Prison Population Brief, England and Wales, 2000 and 2002. Home Office, Research, Development and Statistics Directorate.

6.9 Proportion of prisoners reconvicted within two years who were discharged from custody in 1997, by gender and age group, in England and Wales

Percentages

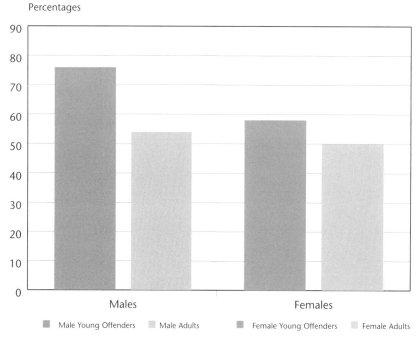

■ Male Young Offenders   ■ Male Adults   ■ Female Young Offenders   ■ Female Adults

SOURCE: Prison Statistics, England and Wales 2000. Home Office, 2001.

The level of disadvantage suffered by this group is a cause for anxiety, as for example the fact that among those aged 15-17 60% had previously been looked after by a local authority. Other risk factors such as low educational attainment and family disruption are common amongst the great majority of young people in custody. One of the most worrying features of this group is the very high proportion coming from black or minority ethnic backgrounds. Data illustrating this can be seen in **Chart 6.10**, which shows that, of a total male young offender population in 1999 of 8,012, 1,064 of these individuals were from a black background. Thus 13% of the male population in young offender institutions is black, compared with 2% in the general population. This is an extremely worrying statistic.

There is no doubt that those young people who receive custodial sentences are highly vulnerable, and much public concern has been expressed over the conditions in which young people are held in prison establishments. To be placed in custody at a young age can be a cause of great distress, especially if the young person is far from home. The situation may be even more difficult if the custodial placement is as a result of a remand rather than a sentence, and it is a shocking fact that between a quarter and a third of all those in custody under the age of 21 are on remand. As with other matters in the youth justice field, this is something that the Youth Justice Board is addressing, although the Board still only has a remit for those under 18. One extreme reflection of the distress experienced by some young people may be seen in self-destructive

6.10 Population of young offenders in prison, by ethnic group and gender, in England and Wales, 1999

Numbers

	Males	Females
White	6,515	255
Black	1064	50
South Asian	245	3
Chinese & Other	183	8
Total	8,012	317

SOURCE: Prison Statistics, England and Wales 2000. Home Office, 2001.

6.11 Numbers of suicides in prison, by age, in England and Wales, 1996-2002

Numbers

Age	1996	1998	1999	2000	2002
16-20	12	15	14	16	12
21-25	14	9	11	14	15
26-30	14	21	21	16	18
31-35	9	17	20	16	16
36-40	5	13	12	8	11
41-45	4	3	9	5	12
46-50	2	2	3	3	5
51-55	2	1	0	2	2
56-60	1	1	1	0	2
60+	1	1	0	1	1
Total	64	83	91	81	94

SOURCE: HM Prison Service Suicide Awareness and Prevention Unit. The Howard League, 2003.

6.12 Psychiatric morbidity among male young offenders

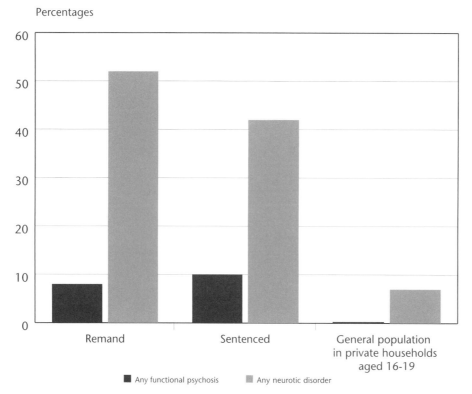

Percentages

SOURCE: Meltzer et al. (1995) and Lader et al. (2000).

6.13 Prevalence of self-reported offending, by age and gender, 2001

Percentages

	Year 7 Boys	Year 7 Girls	Year 8 Boys	Year 8 Girls	Year 9 Boys	Year 9 Girls	Year 10 Boys	Year 10 Girls	Year 11 Boys	Year 11 Girls
Ever stolen anything?	23.2	16.6	31.5	25.2	39.2	36.2	44.0	39.2	43.9	37.4
Shoplifted in last year?	11.4	6.8	18.3	16.6	23.0	24.1	27.6	25.7	25.7	20.3
Stolen/tried to steal a vehicle in last year?	1.1	0.1	2.9	1.0	4.9	0.8	5.9	2.3	7.2	2.0
Stolen/tried to steal from vehicle in last year?	1.4	0.8	3.9	1.0	4.3	1.0	6.1	2.2	6.9	2.0
Stolen/tried to steal something else in last year?	12.7	7.1	15.8	10.2	20.6	14.7	23.3	15.1	18.7	11.1
Broken into building intending to steal in last year?	2.2	0.8	4.8	2.1	6.6	1.6	8.8	3.5	9.7	3.6
Vandalised property in last year?	13.4	8.8	19.3	18.5	24.8	24.2	30.8	32.9	30.0	25.0
Handled stolen food in last year?	7.2	4.4	17.9	11.7	22.1	16.1	28.9	21.6	28.3	18.9
Attacked someone intending harm in last year?	7.8	3.4	13.8	7.4	17.0	7.0	17.3	9	18.9	8.5
Carried weapon in last year?	10.4	2.1	17.8	4.5	20.1	5.0	22.8	6.5	23.6	7.8
Ever sold/dealt drugs?	1.0	0.1	2.6	0.9	4.0	1.9	7.5	6.2	11	5.5
Ever been arrested?	4.2	0.9	7.9	3.7	11.4	4.1	14.8	6.4	13.2	6.8

SOURCE: Risk and Protective Factors associated with Youth Crime and Effective Interventions to Prevent it. Youth Justice Board, 2001.

behaviour. The number of suicides in prison has worried many commentators, and the extent of the problem is illustrated in **Chart 6.11.**

From this it can be seen that the numbers of those up to the age of 30 have stayed relatively stable over the period 1996 to 2002, with some slight changes from year to year. Nonetheless the fact that 12 young people under the age of 20, and a further 15 young adults between the age of 21 and 25, died as a result of suicide in 2002 is an indictment of the custodial system working in England and Wales today. While suicide awareness training has been introduced there is still clearly much more to do if these figures are to be substantially reduced.

The poor mental health of young offenders is a characteristic which has been highlighted in many of the reports mentioned so far in this chapter. One key study to have provided important information is that carried out by Lader et al. (2000). Some results from this research are illustrated in **Chart 6.12.** Figures are only shown for male young offenders, but from these it can be seen that rates of both functional psychosis and neurotic disorders are many times higher in this group than among the population as a whole. The sample of female offenders was too small in most categories to be able to draw any reliable conclusions, but among sentenced young women the rate of neurotic disorder was 68% compared with 19% in the general population. Again these are worrying statistics, and reflect the challenges faced by prison officers and health professionals working in custodial settings.

6.14 Prevalence of self-reported offending in the previous year, by gender and ethnic group, among 12-30 year-olds

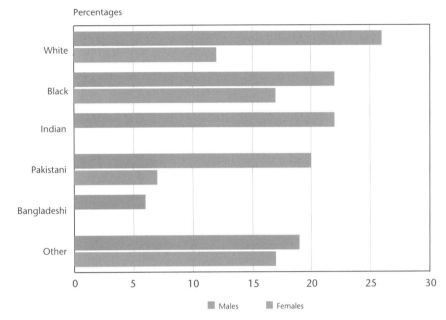

N.B. Less than 1% of Indian and Bangladeshi young women report involvement in offending.

SOURCE: Flood-Page et al. (2000).

6.15 Average number of days from arrest to sentence for persistent young offenders in England and Wales, 1996-2002

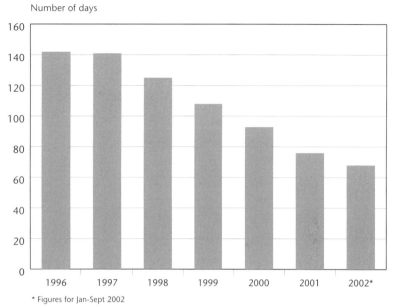

Number of days

* Figures for Jan-Sept 2002

SOURCE: Statistics on Persistent Young Offenders. Lord Chancellor's Department, 2002.

6.16 Young people aged 10-17 sentenced for indictable offences whose parents were ordered to pay fines or compensation, 1996-2001

	Parents to pay fine		Parents to pay compensation	
	Number	As a percentage of all fines	Number	As a percentage of all compensation orders
Males				
1996	364	9	1,983	21
1997	414	9	2,175	24
1998	465	9	2,067	23
1999	552	10	2,091	23
2000	517	10	2,215	25
2001	523	10	2,277	27
Females				
1996	54	11	304	25
1997	56	12	301	24
1998	77	13	364	28
1999	66	10	326	26
2000	96	14	339	26
2001	86	14	386	29

SOURCE: Criminal Statistics, England and Wales, 2001. Research, Development & Statistics Directorate and National Statistics. © Crown Copyright 2002.

Turning now from considerations of custody to more general issues to do with youth crime, it is well-known that statistics in this field are open to all manner of criticism. One charge that is often levelled is that appearances in court are a serious underestimate of the true rate of offending. One way of getting around this problem is to look at self-reported offending behaviour. There have been many studies on this topic in the past few years, but the one we will illustrate here is that reported in a study carried out by Communities that Care and published by the Youth Justice Board in 2001. This study involved 14,500 pupils in secondary schools in England and Wales, and shows rates of self-reported offending in five school year groups relating to various categories of offence. Thus, for example, 25% of boys and 20% of girls aged 15 reported having taken something from a shop in the past year, whilst 23% of boys and 7% of girls reported having carried a weapon of some sort. Full details are shown in **Chart 6.13**.

This study does not show a breakdown according to ethnicity. However the question of whether those from various minority ethnic groups differ in self-reported offending is a very important one, especially in view of the high numbers of black young people within the prison population. One of the most recent self-report studies to have looked at this question is that by Flood-Page et al. (2000), who studied young people and young adults between the ages of 12 and 30. Findings from this study, which are illustrated in **Chart 6.14**, indicate that there are somewhat higher rates of offending among white young men, while there are slightly higher rates among black young women. Some groups, such as Bangladeshis, show very low rates indeed. In sum there is no evidence, at least in this self-report study, to show that there are markedly higher rates of offending among black young people.

A finding which supports this conclusion may be found in the 2002 MORI Survey carried out for the Youth Justice Board. This looked at self-reported offending among school pupils, and showed that 26% of the population in the study reported having offended in the past year. When broken down by ethnicity there was no difference at all between the groups – 26% of white pupils and 26% of minority ethnic group pupils reported offending.

One of the major commitments made by the Youth Justice Board from its earliest days has been the aim of reducing the period between arrest and sentence for young offenders. In the landmark text "Misspent youth: young people and crime" published by the Audit Commission in 1996 much was made of the extremely long time being taken to bring young offenders to sentence. Thus a useful criterion of the success of the Board may be seen in the reduction in the time between arrest and sentence. Data illustrated in **Chart 6.15** show that some considerable progress has been made in this area, and that the average time for this measure in relation to persistent young offenders has been reduced from 142 days in 1996 to 76 days in 2001. The target has been to get the

6.17 Percentage who have been a victim of violence, by age and gender, in Britain, 2001/02

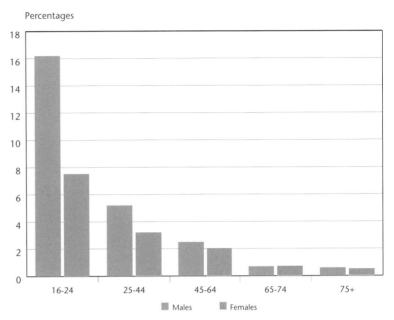

SOURCE: Crime in England and Wales 2001/2002. Home Office Statistical Bulletin, 2002.

6.18 Percentage who have been a victim of burglary, by age, in Britain, 2001/02

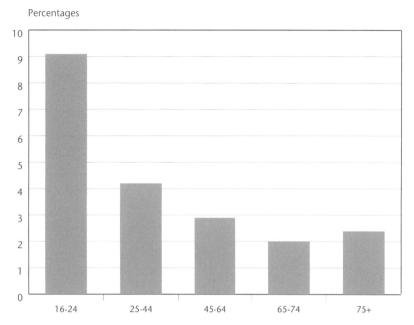

Percentages

SOURCE: Crime in England and Wales 2001/2002. Home Office Statistical Bulletin, 2002.

time down to 71 days or less, and this has been achieved in some months of 2001 and in the first nine months of 2002. Thus a real achievement in this field can be noted. Clearly there is more to do, and it will be interesting to see figures relating not only to those classified as persistent offenders, but to first time and less persistent offenders as well.

Another area of great interest as a result of the youth justice reforms has been the introduction of the Parenting Order, and the very considerable increase in the number of both compulsory and voluntary interventions for parents of young offenders. Apart from a relatively small scale study carried out by the Policy Research Bureau (Ghate and Hazell, 2002) we have as yet little evidence relating to the impact of parenting interventions on offending behaviour. We will need some time yet before we have sufficient evidence to evaluate the impact of the use of these interventions. In the interim we can see how the courts have treated parents in the context of the use of fines and compensation orders. As will be seen from the figures in **Chart 6.16** there has been a small but gradual increase in the use of the option of making parents responsible for paying fines or compensation over the period 1996 to 2001.

Finally in this chapter we will turn to the question of victimization, and to the evidence that young men in particular suffer as victims of crime. Thus not only are males in late adolescence the group most likely to be committing crime, they are also those most likely to be the victims of offences against the person. This can be seen from the data in **Chart 6.17**. From this it will be evident that young men and young women are more likely than any other age group to be the victims of violence. In addition, however, it is worrying to note that they are also most likely to be the victims of other crime, such as burglary. This is shown by the figures in **Chart 6.18**.

To conclude, it will be apparent from this chapter that the field of youth crime has seen a striking amount of activity since 1998 when the youth justice reforms passed into law. A range of new sentences have become available to the courts, the whole process of managing the youth justice procedures, both in the community and in the custodial sector, has changed, targets for the reduction of offending and for delay in dealing with offenders have been put in place, and a number of new reports and research studies have been published. All this is to the good, but it does mean that the field is now much less easy to summarise in one short chapter. Inevitably many interesting features of the activity in this field have been omitted in the cause of brevity and simplicity. The youth justice reforms have opened the way for a new and imaginative approach to offending by young people. With many other commentators we will be watching with great interest the progress of these reforms in the years to come.

References

Flood-Page, C et al. (2000) Youth crime: findings from the 1998/1999 Youth Lifestyles Survey. Home Office Research Study No. 209. RDS Directorate. Home Office.

Ghate, D and Hazell, N (2002) Positive parenting: The national evaluation of the Youth Justice Board's parenting programme. Youth Justice Board. London.

Lader, D et al. (2000) Psychiatric morbidity among young offenders in England and Wales. The Stationery Office. London.

Meltzer, H et al. (1995) The prevalence of psychiatric morbidity among adults living in private households. OPCS Survey of Psychiatric Morbidity in Great Britain: Report 1. The Stationery Office. London.

_____ (1996) Misspent youth: young people and crime. Audit Commission. London.

_____ (2001) Risk and protective factors associated with youth crime and effective interventions to prevent it. Research undertaken by Communities that Care for the Youth Justice Board.

_____ (2002) Youth Survey 2002. MORI research study for the Youth Justice Board.

_____ (2002) Reducing re-offending by ex-prisoners. Report by the Social Exclusion Unit. The Stationery Office. London.

Index